THE HOMEMADE

PIZZA

COOKBOOK BIBLE

Learn the Italian Secrets for Making Perfect Pizza at Home. Discover 1000 Days Mouthwatering Recipes for Every Kind of Homemade Pizza from Neapolitan and Sicilian to New York Style and Chicago Deep Dish. Gluten-Free and Vegan Options Included

Tony Martucci

The Homemade Pizza Cookbook Bible

© Copyright 2023 All rights reserved.

Written by Tony Martucci

Limited Liability - Disclaimer

Please note that the content of this book is based on personal experience and various information sources, and it is only for personal use.

Please note the information contained within this document is for educational and entertainment purposes only and no warranties of any kind are declared or implied.

Readers acknowledge that the author is not engaged in providing medical, dietary, nutritional or professional advice, or physical training. Please consult a doctor, nutritionist or dietician, before attempting any techniques outlined in this book.

Nothing in this book is intended to replace common sense or medical consultation or professional advice and is meant only to inform.

Your particular circumstances may not be suited to the example illustrated in this book; in fact, they likely will not be.

You should use the information in this book at your own risk. The reader is responsible for his or her actions.

The information provided herein is stated to be truthful and consistent, in that any liability, in terms of inattention or otherwise, by any usage or abuse of any policies, processes, or directions contained within is the solitary and utter responsibility of the recipient reader.

By reading this book, the reader agrees that under no circumstances is the author responsible for any losses, direct or indirect, which are incurred as a result of the use of the information contained within this document, including, but not limited to, errors, omissions, or inaccuracies.

TABLE OF CONTENTS

INTRODUCTION

Pizza, oh how I love it! Did you know that pizza has been enjoyed by people for centuries? It's an Italian creation, a delicious flat pie with a face wide open, topped with savory pizza sauce, gooey cheese, and all sorts of tasty meats or veggies. But where did it all begin?

ORIGIN OF PIZZA

Well, way back in the olden days, even before fancy technology and cars, pizza had humble beginnings. Imagine this, my friend - flatbread topped with garlic, lard, and salt. It may not sound like much, but for the poor folks, it was a simple and scrumptious meal. And get this, some creative souls even topped their flatbreads with horseradish cheese, whitebait, or just tomatoes! Can you believe it?

Now, fast forward to the late nineteenth century, and we have a royal pizza connection. King Umberto I and Queen Margherita paid a visit to the Naples Pizzeria Brandi and ordered a bunch of pizzas. The queen had a favorite - the mozzarella cheese pizza, topped with tomatoes and basil. Legend has it that they named it pizza Margherita after her. But it wasn't until the 1940s that pizza truly spread its wings and became a sensation in America, thanks to Neapolitan immigrants recreating their delicious crusty pizzas in cities like New York, Boston, and Chicago. People from all walks of life couldn't resist the flavors and aromas of this heavenly dish. That's when the pizza craze truly took off!

VARIETIES OF PIZZA

Now, let's talk about the different types of pizzas out there. There's a lot more to pizza than meets the eye!

A. Crust Thickness

The thickness of the crust is what sets pizzas apart. You've got thin, medium, and thick crusts to choose from. The amount of dough used plays a big role in determining the thickness. But here's a secret - the rise of the dough matters too. If the dough is under-risen or squished down before baking, you'll end up with a thinner crust. But if you let that dough rise to its full potential before rolling and baking, you'll get a lovely, thicker crust.

B. Round vs. Rectangular Shape

Pizzas come in different shapes too! You've got the classic round pizzas, which are the most common at pizzerias. They're easy to make and enjoy. But guess what? There's also the rectangular pizza, sometimes called Italian bakery pizza. And hey, if you're feeling extra fancy, you can even find specialty shapes like heart-shaped pizzas! Isn't that adorable?

C. Assembly

When it comes to assembling pizzas, there are three main types to know about. First, we've got the deep-dish pizza, like the famous Chicago-style. These pizzas with their thicker crusts are usually baked in a pan. Then there's the peel pizza, which has a thinner crust and is often assembled on a screen or peel. And finally, we have silicon-baked pizzas, which are made and baked on non-burning silicon-treated paper. Now that's some creative pizza-making!

D. Origin

Let's take a little journey around the world of pizza flavors. In Italy, the marinara and Margherita pizzas reign supreme. New York-style pizzas are all about that gooey mozzarella cheese, but they also like to add garlic, various cheeses, anchovies, shrimp, and more. If you're in California, get ready for gourmet flavors that will blow your taste buds away. Now, if you find yourself in Chicago, brace yourself for a crusty and filling experience. Their pizzas have raised edges and are typically loaded with delicious meats. And hey, there are even more unique pizzas from different parts of North America, Asia, Oceania, South America, and Africa. Pizza truly knows no boundaries!

E. Toppings

Ah, the toppings! This is where pizza becomes a canvas for culinary creativity. You can let your imagination run wild and top your pizza with almost anything your heart desires. From juicy meats and poultry to mouthwatering seafood, and even fruits, tofu, and vegetables. The possibilities are endless! You can truly customize your pizza to suit your taste buds.

TYPES OF PIZZA OVENS FOR THE HOME COOK

Now that we know all about the glorious world of pizzas, let's talk about the tools that make it all happen. A good pizza oven is a must for any pizza enthusiast. Here are three popular types of pizza ovens you can consider:

A. BRICK OVENS

If you're aiming for that authentic Italian pizza experience, a brick-style pizza oven is the way to go. These ovens cook pizzas slowly and evenly, just like they do in the old country. You can use wood as fuel, which adds a smoky flavor to your creations. It takes a little time for the oven to heat up, around 45 minutes or so, but once it reaches a blazing temperature of 1000 degrees Fahrenheit, you'll be able to cook a pizza in just 2-3 minutes. Now that's hot stuff!

B. CONVECTION PIZZA OVEN

For those who want a more compact option, convection ovens are like smaller versions of brick ovens. They produce higher heat levels, which means you can bake multiple pizzas at once. And guess what? You can even use them for baking bread, making them a multitasking champ in the kitchen!

C. COUNTERTOP PIZZA OVEN

If you're all about convenience and saving space, a countertop pizza oven is your best friend. These little wonders are perfect for quick and delicious pizza-making at home. They are smaller, less expensive, and super easy to use. Just plug it in, let it heat up, and you'll have a perfectly cooked pizza in as little as 15 minutes. That's a slice of heaven in no time!

PIZZA EQUIPMENT AND ACCESSORIES

Now, let's dive into the tools that will elevate your pizza-making game. With these handy pieces of equipment and accessories, you'll be a pizza pro in no time:

A. **Pizza oven** - There are various types of pizza ovens out there, so choose one that suits your needs and the kind of pizza you want to make.

B. **Dough mixer** - Mixing dough by hand can be quite a workout. That's where a dough mixer comes in. It's a handy machine that takes care of the hard work for you. Look for one with a capacity of around 6 kilograms to handle your pizza-making adventures.

C. **Pizza peel** - Launching your pizza into the oven can be tricky without a pizza peel. It's like a giant spatula that helps you transfer your pizza in and out of the oven without burning yourself. Trust me, it's a lifesaver!

D. **Pizza cutter** - No pizza feast is complete without a trusty pizza cutter. It ensures you get perfect slices every time, without making a mess of the toppings or cheese. Slice away with confidence!

E. **Heat-resistant gloves** - When you're dealing with hot pizza ovens, it's essential to protect your hands. Heat-resistant gloves will be your shield against those scorching temperatures. Safety first!

F. **Pizza Steel** - Want that crispy, light crust? A pizza steel is your secret weapon. It's a special steel plate designed for baking pizzas in a home oven or broiler. It helps create that perfect crust we all crave.

G. **Parchment Paper** - Sometimes, baking your pizza on parchment paper can make the process a breeze. It allows for easy transfer from your pizza peel to the oven, ensuring nothing sticks along the way.

H. **Cast Iron Skillet** - If you're in the mood for a Chicago-style pizza, a cast iron skillet is your best friend. Just brush some oil on its surface, place your stretched dough round in the skillet, add your desired toppings, and let it work its magic in the oven.

With these tools and accessories by your side, you'll be well-equipped to create pizza masterpieces right in your own kitchen. Get ready to impress your friends and family with your culinary skills!

And there you have it, my friend! The delightful world of pizza, from its humble origins to the incredible variety of flavors and the tools that make it all possible. Now, go forth and explore the wonderful world of pizza-making. Enjoy the process, experiment with toppings, and savor every cheesy, saucy bite. Pizza perfection awaits!

CHAPTER 1: PIZZA DOUGH

TRADITIONAL ITALIAN BASIC DOUGH

Experience the authentic taste of Italy with our traditional Italian basic dough, also known as "pasta all'uovo." Passed down through generations, this fundamental element of Italian cuisine has been perfected to bring you the true essence of Italian flavor. Indulge in the authentic flavors of Italy with this versatile dough that serves as the foundation for a variety of beloved dishes. From the classic tagliatelle to the mouth-watering lasagna, ravioli, and tortellini, this dough is the perfect canvas for your culinary creativity.

Experience the true essence of Italian cooking with our dough made from the finest quality flour and eggs. With just a few simple ingredients, we've captured the essence of simplicity and quality that defines Italian cuisine. Experience the art of dough-making as each ingredient comes together in perfect harmony, resulting in a smooth and elastic texture that captures the authentic flavors of Italy.

Crafting the perfect traditional Italian dough demands a meticulous approach, unwavering attention to detail, and a profound reverence for the culinary customs of Italy. For Italians, the art of pasta-making is a treasured aspect of their cultural heritage that has been revered for generations. Experience the deeply gratifying act of kneading dough by hand, feeling its transformation under your fingertips. This time-honored tradition connects generations of Italians and pasta lovers worldwide.

Discover the exquisite allure of this fundamental dough, which boasts not only simplicity but also remarkable versatility. Discover the endless possibilities of pasta as it transforms into a variety of styles, each with its own distinct personality and function. Indulge in the endless possibilities of Italian cuisine with long and ribbon-like tagliatelle, delicate and stuffed ravioli, or layered sheets for comforting lasagna. The options are as vast as the rich Italian culinary tradition itself.

Makes: Dough for 1 Pizza
Preparation Time: 1 hour

Ingredients:
- Olive oil
- 1¼ teaspoons salt
- 1 cup slightly warm water
- ¼ ounce dry yeast
- Pinch sugar
- 2½ cups '00' pizza flour

Instructions:
a) In a bowl, combine warm water and yeast. Whisk the mixture until the yeast is completely dissolved.
b) In a mixing bowl, combine salt, flour, and sugar until the dough comes together.
c) Drizzle the dough with olive oil.
d) Cover the bowl using either plastic wrap or a kitchen towel.
e) Allow the dough to rise by setting it aside for an hour.

GLUTEN-FREE PIZZA DOUGH

Discover a world of possibilities with gluten-free pizza dough! Perfect for those with dietary restrictions or who choose to avoid gluten. Indulge in a mouth-watering and fulfilling gluten-free pizza crust that doesn't sacrifice flavor or consistency, unlike the conventional dough that depends on gluten for its flexibility and form.

Experience the perfect gluten-free pizza crust by selecting and combining the finest ingredients with precision and care. Achieve the desired consistency and flavor that will leave your taste buds craving for more. Indulge in the goodness of gluten-free flours such as rice flour, almond flour, tapioca flour, or a harmonious blend of multiple flours that culminate into a delectable and well-rounded base. Experience the perfect balance of structure and flavor with our premium selection of flours. Each variety brings its own distinct qualities to your baking, ensuring a truly exceptional result every time.

Achieving elasticity in gluten-free dough can be challenging due to the absence of gluten. Achieving the perfect texture in gluten-free recipes can be a challenge, but fear not! We have the solution. By incorporating binding agents such as xanthan gum, psyllium husk, or flaxseed meal, you can effortlessly mimic the stretch and pliability that gluten provides. Indulge in the perfect dough by adding eggs, olive oil, or dairy-free alternatives to elevate its texture, taste, and moisture content.

Indulge in the delicious taste of pizza without any worries! Our gluten-free pizza dough is the perfect solution for those with gluten sensitivities, celiac disease, or anyone following a gluten-free lifestyle. Savor every bite without any adverse effects. Indulge in a world of culinary possibilities with our versatile canvas, perfect for a plethora of creative toppings. From the timeless Margherita to the more daring and gourmet options, elevate your taste buds with every bite.

Makes: Dough for 1 Large Pizza
Preparation Time: 72 hours, 15 minutes

Ingredients:
- 1 tablespoon yeast
- 1½ teaspoons salt
- 3 cups gluten-free flour
- 4½ tablespoons extra-virgin olive oil
- 1½ teaspoons sugar
- 1⅛ cups slightly warm water

Instructions:
a) In a mixing bowl, mix together flour, yeast, salt, and sugar.

b) To prepare the dough, mix the dry ingredients with water and oil until a firm dough is formed.

c) Using a stand mixer, mix the dough on high speed for three minutes.

d) Lightly spray the dough with cooking oil. Then tightly cover the dough in an oiled container.

e) Let the dough rise for approximately one hour until it has expanded to 150% of its initial volume.

SOURDOUGH PIZZA DOUGH

Sourdough pizza dough embodies the marriage of two culinary delights: the distinct tangy flavor of sourdough and the beloved classic of pizza. Elevate your pizza-making game with our artisanal dough that promises a one-of-a-kind taste experience. Our naturally leavened bread boasts a depth and complexity that will leave your taste buds wanting more.

Sourdough pizza dough starts with a sourdough starter, a living culture of wild yeast and bacteria that ferments flour and water over time, creating a natural leavening agent. Experience the perfect rise and tangy flavor of our dough, while also enjoying its enhanced digestibility and nutritional benefits.

Experience the art of sourdough pizza making with our expertly crafted dough that is made with patience and precision. The starter is carefully nurtured and fed, allowing it to grow and become active. Crafting the perfect dough requires the perfect combination of ingredients. By skillfully blending a portion of the starter with flour, water, and salt, a robust and flavorful base is created. The dough is then left to ferment for several hours or even overnight, allowing the wild yeast and bacteria to work their magic, imparting the dough with its unique taste and texture.

What sets sourdough pizza dough apart is its depth of flavor and its characteristic chewiness. The long fermentation process not only develops the dough's distinct tang but also helps break down complex carbohydrates and proteins, resulting in a more easily digestible crust. Experience the perfect texture and crust with our slow-rise and fermented dough. Baked at high temperatures, our pizza boasts an airy texture and a beautifully blistered crust.

Indulge in the culinary artistry of sourdough pizza dough, where a plethora of toppings can be masterfully combined to create a symphony of flavors that perfectly complement the intricate texture of the crust. Indulge in a variety of delectable pizza options, ranging from classic margherita with fresh mozzarella and basil to bold and daring combinations such as prosciutto and arugula or roasted vegetables with goat cheese. The options are truly limitless!

Making sourdough pizza dough is a labor of love, requiring dedication and an understanding of the fermentation process. It is a testament to the artistry and craftsmanship of baking, marrying the ancient traditions of sourdough with the universal appeal of pizza. Indulge in a slice of pizza that goes beyond the norm, providing a sensory journey that will excite your taste buds and fulfill your deepest cravings.

Embark on a tantalizing journey of sourdough pizza-making, where you can unleash your creativity by experimenting with an array of flours, toppings, and fermentation times to craft your very own signature crust. Indulge in the perfect combination of tradition, flavor, and artistry with sourdough pizza dough. Whether you're a seasoned sourdough aficionado or a pizza lover seeking to elevate your culinary adventures, this delectable option is guaranteed to leave a lasting impression.

Makes: Dough for 1 Large Pizza
Preparation Time: 24 hours

Ingredients:
- 1¾ teaspoons salt
- 1½ cups water
- ¾ cups sourdough starter
- 4 cups all-purpose or bread flour

Instructions:
a) Whisk the sourdough starter, salt, and water together.
b) Add the flour into the mixture.
c) Transfer the dough to a container with straight sides.
d) Place a clean cloth over the container and allow it to rest for 30 minutes.

WHOLE GRAIN PIZZA DOUGH

Indulge in a wholesome twist on the classic pizza with our whole grain pizza dough. Every bite is infused with the goodness of whole grains, making it a guilt-free indulgence. Indulge in a guilt-free pizza experience with our wholesome pizza crust made from all-natural ingredients. It's a delicious testament to the increasing recognition and value of incorporating whole foods into our daily meals.

Indulge in the wholesome goodness of our pizza dough made with a medley of whole grain flours like whole wheat, spelt, rye, or a combination of various grains. Say goodbye to refined flours and savor the rich flavors of our whole grain pizza dough. Experience the full potential of your baked goods with our nutrient-packed flours. Our products retain the wholesome bran and germ, providing a richer fiber content, elevated levels of essential vitamins and minerals, and a more intricate flavor profile compared to ordinary refined flours.

Experience the perfect balance of flavors and textures with our expertly crafted whole grain pizza dough. Experience the rich and distinct flavor of our dough, enhanced by the addition of whole grain flours. Each slice is imbued with a nutty and earthy essence that adds depth and character to your culinary creations. Indulge in the delightful texture of our crust, crafted with fiber-rich bran that adds a touch of density and heartiness. Satisfy your cravings with a crust that offers a satisfying chew.

Indulge in the rich diversity of grains with our whole grain pizza dough that paves the way for endless creative possibilities. Indulge in a world of flavor possibilities with our pizza options, ranging from the timeless Margherita to the daring toppings of roasted veggies, tangy goat cheese, or the sweet and savory combo of figs and prosciutto. The door to culinary exploration is wide open. Indulge in a truly satisfying pizza experience with our whole grain dough that boasts robust flavors. Whether you prefer classic or unique toppings, our dough perfectly complements them all. Plus, you can enjoy the added benefit of a healthier option without sacrificing taste.

Experience the elevated taste and texture of your pizza by choosing whole grain pizza dough. Not only that, but you'll also be contributing to a well-rounded and balanced diet. Experience sustained energy, improved digestion, and enhanced overall well-being with the addition of whole grains to your diet. These nutrient-rich grains provide essential vitamins and minerals to fuel your body and keep you feeling your best.

Embark on a culinary journey that embraces both flavor and nutrition by indulging in our whole grain pizza dough. Indulge in the pleasures of pizza-making while nourishing your body with every delectable bite. Indulge in a guilt-free pizza experience with our hearty crust, earthy aromas, and wholesome ingredients. Savor every bite knowing you've made a gratifying and healthy choice.

Makes: Dough for 1 12-inch pizza
Preparation Time: 2 hours, 15 minutes

Ingredients:
- ¾ cup slightly warm water
- ½ teaspoon salt
- 1 tablespoon extra-virgin olive oil
- ½ cup yeast
- ½ cup honey
- 1¼ cups whole wheat flour

Instructions
a) Whisk together honey, yeast, and water and allow the mixture to rest for 5 minutes until a layer of foam forms on the surface.
b) Add olive oil, flour, and salt to the mixture.
c) Beat the dough on low speed in a mixer for about 3-4 minutes.
d) Get the dough out of the mixture and knead it with lightly floured hands.
e) Coat the dough with oil and place it in an oiled bowl.
f) Cover the bowl with aluminum foil or a kitchen towel and let it rise for 2 hours.

MULTIGRAIN PIZZA DOUGH

Multigrain pizza dough takes the concept of whole grain dough to the next level, incorporating a medley of diverse grains and seeds for a truly wholesome and flavorful pizza experience. This innovative twist on traditional pizza dough offers a delightful blend of textures, tastes, and nutritional benefits that showcase the richness of a variety of grains.

Multigrain pizza dough combines different whole grain flours, such as whole wheat, spelt, cornmeal, barley, or oats, along with an array of seeds such as flaxseeds, chia seeds, or sesame seeds. Each grain and seed brings its own unique flavor, texture, and nutritional profile, resulting in a complex and satisfying crust that is both delicious and nourishing.

Crafting multigrain pizza dough requires careful consideration of the proportions and combinations of grains and seeds to achieve the desired taste and texture. The inclusion of different grains adds depth and complexity to the dough, while the addition of seeds brings a delightful crunch and boosts the nutritional value with their abundance of healthy fats, fiber, and minerals.

The multigrain pizza dough opens up a world of creative possibilities, allowing you to experiment with a wide range of flavors and toppings. From classic combinations like a margherita or pepperoni to more adventurous choices like roasted vegetables, feta cheese, or caramelized onions, the multigrain crust provides a sturdy base that complements and enhances the flavors of the toppings.

Choosing multigrain pizza dough not only offers a delightful culinary experience but also provides numerous health benefits. The combination of whole grains and seeds introduces a wealth of nutrients, including fiber, vitamins, minerals, and antioxidants. These elements promote digestion, support heart health, and contribute to overall well-being.

By embracing multigrain pizza dough, you embark on a journey that celebrates the diversity and nutritional value of different grains and seeds. Each slice becomes a canvas for exploring flavors, textures, and the endless possibilities of a well-rounded and nourishing meal.

Makes: Dough for 1 Large Pizza
Preparation Time: 1 hour 20 mins

Ingredients:
- 1 cup slightly warm water
- 2 tablespoons whole-wheat flour
- 2 cups maize flour
- 1 tablespoon olive oil
- 2 tablespoons whole-wheat flour
- 2 tablespoons yeast
- 1 tablespoon oatmeal
- 1 cup sunflower seeds
- 1 tablespoon sugar

Instructions
a) Mix slightly warm water and sugar together.
b) Sprinkle active yeast over the water, cover, and set aside for 20 minutes.
c) Mix sunflower seeds, whole wheat flour, oats, maize flour, flax seed powder, olive oil, and yeast water.
d) Knead the dough until it becomes glossy and smooth, then set it aside for 1 hour.

CHAPTER 2: MEAT PIZZA

1) *Four Seasons Pizza/Quattro Stagioni*

Indulge in the timeless and visually captivating Four Seasons Pizza, also known as "Quattro Stagioni" in its native Italian. This pizza masterpiece artfully captures the essence of each season through its carefully selected toppings. Experience the essence of Italy with our beloved creation, divided into four sections, each adorned with distinct ingredients that reflect the flavors and colors of the seasons. From the freshness of spring to the warmth of summer, the richness of autumn, and the comfort of winter, indulge in the flavors of the Italian countryside. Indulge in the classic Quattro Stagioni pizza, complete with a delectable circular dough base and a tantalizing dividing line of tomato sauce or, for the adventurous, pesto. Experience the four quadrants, each adorned with a unique selection of toppings that perfectly embody the essence of each season.

Makes: 1 Large Pizza
Baking Time: about 18 Minutes

Ingredients:

- 1 recipe for Traditional Italian basic Dough
- 6 ounces of Mozzarella, sliced
- 3 ounces of Prosciutto, sliced
- 1 cup of sliced Shiitake mushrooms
- ½ cup of Olives, sliced
- ½ cup of Pizza Sauce
- 1 cup of Quartered artichoke hearts
- 2 ounces of Grated Parmigiano

Instructions:

a) Shape the dough into a 14-inch circle by gently stretching and rotating the edges.
b) Evenly spread the pizza sauce over the dough.
c) Place the sliced mozzarella on top of the sauce.
d) Divide the pizza into four quarters and top each quarter with artichoke hearts, prosciutto, mushrooms, and olives.
e) Sprinkle grated Parmigiano on top.
f) Grill or bake for approximately 18 minutes.

2) *BLT Pizza*

Experience the ultimate indulgence with our BLT Pizza, a mouthwatering fusion of classic BLT sandwich flavors and the irresistible goodness of pizza. Indulge in the ultimate taste sensation with our irresistible pizza creation. Savor the perfect combination of crispy bacon, fresh lettuce, and juicy tomatoes, all atop a delectable pizza crust. This mouthwatering masterpiece is a delightful twist on two classic favorites that will leave you craving more.

Indulge in the mouth-watering BLT Pizza, crafted with a classic pizza base that boasts a thin or medium-thick crust. Indulge in the perfect foundation for your dish with a layer of tangy tomato sauce or a creamy base like mayonnaise or ranch dressing. Indulge in the mouthwatering goodness of our pizza, generously topped with crispy bacon strips that add a savory and smoky element to every bite. Next comes the vibrant lettuce, adding a refreshing crunch and a touch of greenery. Experience the perfect pizza with our crisp and juicy tomato slices, adding a burst of bright and summery flavors to complete the trio. Elevate your culinary experience with a variety of toppings such as savory shredded cheese, zesty red onions, or a delicate sprinkle of herbs to add depth and dimension to your dish.

Makes: 1 Large Pizza
Baking Time: about 18 Minutes

Ingredients:
- 1 recipe for Traditional Italian basic Dough
- 12 ounces of crispy bacon strips, diced
- 2 tablespoons mayonnaise
- 2 teaspoons lemon juice
- 6 ounces of Mozzarella, shredded
- 1 beefsteak tomato, diced
- 1½ tablespoons Dijon mustard, plus 1 teaspoon
- 1 teaspoon Worcestershire sauce
- 2 cups shredded iceberg lettuce
- 2 cups shredded iceberg lettuce

Instructions:
a) Shape the dough into a 14-inch circle by gently stretching and rotating the edges.
b) Spread half of the mustard on top of the crust.
c) Scatter shredded mozzarella, diced tomato, and chopped bacon on top.
d) Grill or bake for about 18 minutes.
e) In a separate bowl, mix the remaining mustard, Worcestershire sauce, lemon juice, and mayonnaise.
f) Add the lettuce to the bowl and toss to coat completely.
g) Slice the pizza into wedges and top each slice with the dressed salad before serving.

3) *Alsatian Tarte Flambé*

Indulge in the mouth-watering delight of Alsatian Tarte Flambé, famously known as Flammkuchen, originating from the picturesque Alsace region of France. This delectable specialty has garnered a global fan following for its exquisite taste and unique flavors. Experience the rich culinary heritage and unique flavors of the region with this rustic and savory delight.

Indulge in the delectable Alsatian Tarte Flambé, boasting a thin and crispy crust that sets the stage for a mouthwatering and uncomplicated topping. Indulge in the classic base of crème fraîche, delicately sliced onions, and savory lardons (smoked bacon). Experience a symphony of flavors with the perfect combination of creamy, smoky, and slightly sweet ingredients.

Indulge in the delectable flavors of our tart, baked to perfection in a hot oven until the crust boasts a golden-brown hue and the topping is tantalizingly caramelized. Indulge in a mouthwatering medley of textures that will leave your taste buds begging for more. The crispy crust offers a delightful crunch, while the delectable toppings provide a savory and comforting sensation that will warm your soul.

Makes: 1 Large Pizza
Baking Time: 16 to 18 minutes

Ingredients:
- 1 recipe for Traditional Italian basic Dough
- 1 yellow onion, sliced
- ¼ teaspoon cracked black pepper
- ¼ cup dry white wine
- 6 ounces of cooked bacon strips, chopped
- 1 cup Crème fraîche
- ¼ teaspoon ground nutmeg

Instructions:
a) Shape the dough into a 14-inch circle by gently stretching and rotating the edges.
b) In a pan, sauté the sliced onions until golden.
c) Add the dry wine and simmer for 4 minutes.
d) Spread the Crème fraîche on top of the prepared crust.
e) Scatter the chopped bacon on top.
f) Scatter the onions over the pizza.
g) Sprinkle with black pepper and nutmeg.
h) Grill or bake for 16 to 18 minutes.

4) *California Pizza*

Experience the vibrant and innovative twist on traditional Italian pizza with California Pizza, also known as California-style pizza. Experience the true essence of California cuisine with this culinary masterpiece that celebrates the state's diverse flavors, fresh ingredients, and unparalleled creativity. Hailing from the Golden State, this dish is a true embodiment of its culinary heritage.

Experience the exceptional taste of California Pizza's distinct toppings, daring flavor fusions, and delightfully crispy thin crust. Experience a pizza like no other, where creativity knows no bounds. Our unconventional take on this classic dish breaks away from the traditional tomato sauce and mozzarella cheese, inviting a wide range of imaginative and non-traditional ingredients to adorn every slice.

Experience the essence of California with our pizzas, where fresh and seasonal produce takes center stage. Vibrant vegetables, fragrant herbs, and succulent fruits steal the spotlight, delivering a revitalizing and nourishing touch to the pizza. Indulge in the vibrant flavors of our toppings, which showcase the bountiful selection of locally-sourced, farm-fresh ingredients. From succulent sun-ripened tomatoes to creamy avocado slices, crisp baby greens, smoky roasted peppers, and savory caramelized onions, our toppings are a celebration of the season's harvest.

Makes: 1 Large Pizza
Baking Time: about 10 minutes

Ingredients:

PESTO
- ½ cup freshly grated Parmesan cheese
- 1 cup olive oil
- 2 cups basil leaves
- 3 tablespoons pine nuts
- 2 cloves garlic, chopped

TOPPINGS
- 3 ounces of goat cheese
- 10 ounces of coarsely grated Mozzarella cheese
- 2 bell peppers, sliced
- 2 tablespoons freshly grated Parmesan cheese
- ½ pound Italian sausage
- 2 tablespoons cornmeal
- 1 onion, sliced
- 2 tablespoons olive oil

Instructions:
a) To make the pesto, blend all the ingredients in a blender until smooth, then stir in the grated Parmesan cheese.
b) Sauté the sliced bell peppers and onions in olive oil until soft.
c) Cook the Italian sausage in a separate pan until browned, then chop into small pieces.
d) Preheat the oven to 450°F (230°C) and lightly oil a pizza pan, then sprinkle cornmeal on top.
e) Roll out the pizza dough with a rolling pin and press it into the pan.
f) Pre-bake the dough for 5 minutes in the preheated oven.
g) Spread the pesto sauce evenly over the dough.
h) Sprinkle goat cheese on top of the pesto.
i) Add the remaining cheeses, sausage, peppers, and onions.
j) Bake for 10 minutes.

5) *New Orleans Style Pizza*

Experience the bold and lively taste of the Large Easy with New Orleans Style Pizza. Experience the indulgent and unique flavors of New Orleans' diverse culinary traditions with our pizza style that perfectly captures the spirit of the city's renowned cuisine.
Indulge in the unique flavor and texture of New Orleans Style Pizza, distinguished by its thick and doughy crust that sets it apart from the ordinary thin-crust pies. Indulge in the decadent and velvety crust that serves as the foundation for the mouth-watering pizza. Its buttery texture offers a sturdy support for the bold and robust toppings that elevate the flavors to new heights.
Indulge in the delectable toppings of New Orleans Style Pizza, a true tribute to the irresistible flavors that have made the city's cuisine a beloved culinary sensation. Indulge in a burst of bold and zesty flavors with our dish featuring Andouille sausage, Cajun-seasoned chicken, shrimp, and crawfish. These ingredients pay homage to the rich Creole and Cajun influences of the region, making every bite a savory delight.

Makes: 1 Large Pizza
Baking Time: about 10 minutes

Ingredients:
- 1 pizza crust
- 2 cloves garlic, chopped
- 8 pitted black olives
- 2 ounces grated Parmesan cheese
- 8 pitted green olives
- 4 ounces sliced prosciutto
- 2 tablespoons chopped onion
- ½ teaspoon dried oregano
- 6 leaves fresh basil, chopped
- 2 ounces salami, sliced
- 2 ounces Mozzarella cheese
- 2 tablespoons chopped celery
- 1 tablespoon chopped fresh parsley
- 2 tablespoons olive oil
- Salt and cracked black pepper, to taste

Instructions:
a) Combine all the ingredients except the cheese in a blender and spread the mixture on top of the pizza crust.
b) Preheat the oven to 500°F (260°C) and bake the pizza for approximately 5 minutes.
c) Sprinkle the grated cheese on top and broil for 5 more minutes.
d) Slice the pizza and serve.

6) *Garden Basil Pepperoni Pizza*

Indulge in the perfect combination of fresh and savory with our Garden Basil Pepperoni Pizza. Savor the vibrant flavors of a garden-fresh salad, perfectly paired with the irresistible indulgence of pepperoni pizza. Indulge in the ultimate pizza experience with this delectable masterpiece. Featuring a rich tomato sauce and melted cheese, this classic recipe is elevated with a medley of fresh garden toppings that will tantalize your taste buds. Experience the true star of the show - fragrant and aromatic basil leaves that add a delightful herbal note to every single bite. Indulge in the perfect harmony of flavors with our pepperoni pizza. The savory and slightly spicy pepperoni slices are perfectly paired with fresh greens, satisfying both pizza and salad enthusiasts. Indulge in the perfect blend of freshness and decadence with our Garden Basil Pepperoni Pizza. Experience the best of both worlds in every delicious slice.

Makes: 4
Baking Time: 10 to 15 minutes

Ingredients:
- ½ pound No-Knead Bread and Pizza Dough
- 1 tablespoon Extra-virgin olive oil
- 1 cup grated Provolone cheese
- 2 cups Cherry tomatoes
- 1 cup grated Mozzarella cheese
- ¾ cup Canned crushed tomatoes
- 8 slices Pepperoni
- 1 garlic clove, chopped or grated
- Salt and freshly cracked pepper, to taste
- Fresh basil, for garnish

Instructions:
a) Roll out the dough on a floured surface.
b) Transfer the dough to a prepared sheet pan.
c) Layer the grated Mozzarella, Provolone, and crushed tomatoes on top.
d) Arrange the pepperoni evenly on the pizza.
e) In a separate bowl, combine cherry tomatoes, garlic, olive oil, salt, and pepper.
f) Spread the cherry tomato mixture evenly over the pizza.
g) Bake the pizza at 450°F (230°C) for 10 to 15 minutes.
h) Garnish with fresh basil leaves.
i) Slice and serve.

7) *Beef and Mushroom Pizza*

Indulge in the ultimate pizza experience with our Beef and Mushroom Pizza. This mouthwatering delight is perfect for those who crave the rich and savory flavors of beef and the earthy goodness of mushrooms. Satisfy your cravings and treat yourself to a hearty and fulfilling meal. Indulge in a mouthwatering masterpiece that harmoniously blends succulent, expertly seasoned beef with rich and savory mushrooms. Savor the explosion of flavors in every bite. Indulge in the classic pizza experience with a luscious tomato sauce and a generous layer of melted cheese, creating a delectable and savory foundation. Experience a new level of flavor with our seasoned beef and mushroom dish. The beef adds a rich depth to the dish, while the mushrooms provide a meaty texture and earthy aroma that perfectly complements the other ingredients. Indulge in the ultimate culinary delight with our Beef and Mushroom Pizza. This delectable dish is perfect for a hearty main course or for sharing with your loved ones. Experience the rich and savory flavors of tender beef and earthy mushrooms that are sure to leave you feeling satisfied and comforted.

Makes: 1 Large Pizza
Baking Time: 16 to 18 minutes

Ingredients:
- 1 recipe for Traditional Italian basic Dough
- 1 tablespoon chopped Parsley leaves
- 1 yellow onion, chopped
- 2 tablespoons Dry sherry
- 8 ounces Lean ground beef
- 1 teaspoon chopped Sage leaves
- 2 tablespoons Steak sauce
- 5 ounces Cremini mushrooms, sliced
- 2 teaspoons Worcestershire sauce
- 1 tablespoon Butter
- 1 teaspoon stemmed Thyme leaves
- ½ teaspoon Salt
- ½ teaspoon freshly cracked Black pepper
- 6 ounces shredded Cheddar cheese

Instructions:
a) Shape the dough into a 14-inch circle by gently stretching and rotating the edges.
b) In a skillet, melt butter and cook chopped onion until softened.
c) Add sliced mushrooms and cook for approximately 5 minutes.
d) In a separate skillet, cook ground beef until browned.
e) Season the beef with salt, pepper, parsley, Worcestershire sauce, sage, and sherry.
f) Spread steak sauce evenly over the crust.
g) Sprinkle shredded Cheddar cheese on top.
h) Distribute the cooked beef mixture and sautéed mushrooms over the cheese.
i) Grill or bake for 16 to 18 minutes.

8) *Spanish Chorizo Pizza*

Experience the bold and robust flavors of Spanish cuisine with our Spanish Chorizo Pizza. Infused with the smoky, spicy, and tangy characteristics of chorizo, this traditional pizza is sure to tantalize your taste buds. Indulge in a mouthwatering pizza that pays homage to the vibrant and bold flavors of Spain. Featuring a delectable tomato sauce base, this pizza is generously topped with a medley of savory ingredients, including sliced chorizo sausage, roasted red peppers, onions, and occasionally, even Manchego cheese. Savor every bite of this Spanish-inspired masterpiece. Indulge in the rich and bold taste of smoky chorizo infused with paprika. Experience a burst of flavor with every bite. The perfect balance of sweetness and depth is achieved with the combination of roasted peppers and onions. Indulge in a mouth-watering pizza that will take your taste buds on a journey to the bustling streets of Spain with every delectable bite. Embark on a culinary journey that is both satisfying and full of zest with Spanish Chorizo Pizza. Whether you're a fan of Spanish cuisine or seeking an adventurous twist on traditional pizza, this dish is sure to delight your taste buds.

Makes: 1 Large Pizza
Baking Time: 10-15 minutes

Ingredients:
- 1 recipe for Traditional Italian basic Dough
- ½ cup Sliced pitted green olives
- 1 red bell pepper, charred and cubed
- Sun-dried tomatoes, in oil
- 6 ounces shredded Mozzarella cheese
- 4 ounces sliced Spanish chorizo
- 1 garlic clove, quartered
- 3 ounces Shaved Manchego or Parmigiano

Instructions:
a) Blend the red pepper, sun-dried tomatoes, and garlic until fairly smooth.
b) Spread the red pepper and sun-dried tomato blend evenly over the prepared crust.
c) Layer the shredded Mozzarella and chorizo slices on top.
d) Scatter the olives over the pizza and distribute the Manchego cheese.
e) Bake the pizza for approximately 15 minutes.

9) *Cream of Pizza*

Indulge in the ultimate pizza experience with Cream of Pizza. Elevating the classic dish to new heights, this luxurious and creamy variation is a must-try for all cheese enthusiasts. Indulge in a one-of-a-kind pizza experience with our signature style that boasts a luscious and smooth foundation crafted from a medley of delectable components like Alfredo sauce, cream sauce infused with garlic, or a fusion of melted cheeses. The creaminess of the base is complemented by a variety of toppings, which can range from classic choices like ham and mushrooms to more gourmet options like caramelized onions, spinach, or even truffle oil. Indulge in a luscious and decadent experience with Cream of Pizza. Our menu showcases the versatility of pizza as a canvas for creative and indulgent flavor combinations. Indulge in the creamy and luxurious side of the beloved pizza dish with Cream of Pizza. Whether it's a special treat or a centerpiece for a sophisticated gathering, savor every moment with this delectable delight.

Makes: 2 Pizzas
Baking Time: 25-30 minutes

Ingredients:
- 2 recipes for Traditional Italian basic Dough
- ¾ cup Milk
- 10¾ ounces Condensed cream of celery soup
- 1 pound Ground sausage
- 1 Onion, chopped
- 12 Eggs
- 3 ounces Canned bacon bits
- 4 cups Shredded Cheddar cheese
- Salt and pepper
- 1 Green bell pepper, chopped

Instructions:
a) Cook ground sausage in a skillet until browned, breaking it apart.
b) In a mixing bowl, combine milk, eggs, black pepper, salt, and sugar.
c) Preheat the oven to 400°F (200°C).
d) Invert the pizza crusts onto baking sheets.
e) Spread the cream of celery soup evenly on top of each crust.
f) Distribute half of the egg mixture onto each crust.
g) Spread canned bacon bits on one pizza and crumbled sausage on the other.
h) Top each pizza with 2 cups of shredded Cheddar cheese, chopped onions, and chopped green bell peppers.
i) Bake for approximately 25 to 30 minutes until the crust is golden and the cheese is melted and bubbly.
j) Allow the pizzas to cool for a few minutes before serving.

10) *Thursday Night Pizza*

Experience the joy and comfort of a weekly tradition with Thursday Night Pizza. It's more than just a meal, it's a highlight that brings households together around the world. Looking for a scrumptious way to kick off your weekend? Look no further than Thursday Night Pizza! Our mouth-watering pies are the perfect way to unwind and celebrate the start of the weekend. Indulge in the cherished custom of crafting your own pizza with your loved ones. This delightful tradition offers a plethora of options, allowing you to personalize your pie with your preferred toppings. Gather your closest companions and savor the experience of customizing your very own pizza. At Thursday Night Pizza, we believe in the power of personalization. Whether you prefer classic toppings like pepperoni, mushrooms, and onions or crave something more adventurous like barbecue chicken, pineapple, and jalapeños, we've got you covered. Let your taste buds run wild and experiment with our delicious pizza combinations. Experience the joy of coming together as you knead dough, spread sauce, and sprinkle cheese. Create a sense of togetherness and excitement that will leave you eagerly anticipating your next gathering. Experience the excitement and pleasure of the upcoming weekend with Thursday Night Pizza - a beloved tradition among pizza enthusiasts, whether shared with dear ones or savored solo.

Makes: 1 Large Pizza
Baking Time: 10-15 minutes

Ingredients:
- 1 recipe for Traditional Italian basic Dough
- ⅓ cup Salsa
- 6 ounces Canned tomato paste
- 4 cups Shredded Cheddar cheese
- ¾ cup Water
- 1¼ ounces Taco seasoning mix, divided
- 16 ounces Canned refried beans
- 1 teaspoon Chili powder
- ½ pound Ground beef
- ½ teaspoon Cayenne pepper
- ¼ cup Chopped onion

Instructions:
a) Combine tomato paste, water, cayenne pepper, chili powder, and ¾ of the taco seasoning mix in a bowl.
b) In a separate bowl, combine salsa, refried beans, and chopped onion.
c) Pan-fry ground beef until fully cooked.
d) Mix the remaining taco seasoning package and water with the ground beef in a skillet. Simmer for a few minutes.
e) Preheat the oven to 400°F (200°C).
f) Divide the dough into two equal portions and press each into a 12-inch baking dish.
g) Layer the bean mixture, beef mixture, shredded Cheddar cheese, and tomato paste mixture over each dough disk.
h) Bake the pizza for 10 to 15 minutes until the crust is golden and the cheese is melted and bubbly.
i) Allow the pizza to cool for a few minutes, then slice and serve.

11) *Meatball Pizza*

Indulge in the ultimate fusion of two American classics with our Philly Cheesesteak Pizza. This mouth-watering masterpiece draws inspiration from the iconic Philadelphia sandwich and elevates it to a whole new level of deliciousness. Indulge in the mouthwatering flavors of the iconic Philly Cheesesteak with our delectable pizza. Featuring succulent, thinly sliced beef, sautéed onions, and gooey melted cheese, every bite is a savory sensation. Indulge in a delectable combination of savory toppings atop a sturdy pizza crust that perfectly complements each bite. Indulge in a mouthwatering experience with every bite of our savory beef sandwich. The sweet onions and gooey melted cheese perfectly complement the rich flavors and textures, creating a symphony of taste that will leave you craving more. Indulge in the savory and satisfying flavors of Philly Cheesesteak Pizza, a culinary tribute to the classic Philly Cheesesteak and the rich traditions of Philadelphia. Whether you're a die-hard fan or simply seeking a deliciously indulgent pizza experience, this dish is sure to delight your taste buds with its bold and flavorful profile.

Makes: 1 Large Pizza
Baking Time: 16 to 18 minutes

Ingredients:

- 1 recipe for Traditional Italian basic Dough
- 8 ounces of Lean ground beef
- 2 table spoons Dried bread crumbs
- ¼ tea spoon Cracked black pepper
- 6 ounces of Shredded mozzarella
- ½ ounce Grated Asiago, Grana Padano, or Pecorino
- 1 tea spoon Fried oregano
- ¼ tea spoon Red pepper flakes
- ¼ tea spoon Salt
- 1 tea spoon Stemmed thyme leaves

- ¼ cup of Chopped parsley leaves
- ½ tea spoon Fennel seeds
- 5 Garlic cloves, chopped
- ¼ tea spoon Ground cloves
- 1 table spoon Olive oil
- 2 ounces of Shaved Parmigiano-Reggiano
- 1 Yellow onion, chopped
- 14-ounce Canned crushed tomatoes
- ¼ tea spoon Grated or ground nutmeg

Instructions:

a) To shape the dough, hold the edges and carefully rotate and stretch it into a 14-inch-diameter circle.
b) To prepare the meat mixture, combine ground beef, parsley, bread crumbs, grated cheese, fried oregano, fennel seeds, salt, black pepper, half of the chopped garlic, and ground cloves in a bowl.
c) Take the mixture and form it into 10 meatballs.
d) Take a skillet and put it on the stove. Pour olive oil into the skillet. Turn on the heat and let the oil heat up.
e) To the skillet, add the remaining chopped garlic cloves and chopped onion. Cook for 3 minutes while stirring frequently.
f) Heat a skillet over medium heat. Then add the crushed tomatoes to the skillet. add the salt, black pepper, grated nutmeg, red pepper flakes, and stemmed thyme leaves to the skillet. Stir the ingredients together. Continue cooking the mixture until heated through.
g) Simmer for a period of time.
h) Preheat the grill or oven to the highest temperature.
i) Spread shredded mozzarella cheese evenly over the pizza crust.
j) Take the meatballs out of the oven. Using a spoon, scoop the tomato sauce from the meatballs. Pour the tomato sauce on top of the cheese.
k) Split each meatball in half. Distribute the halves evenly throughout the pizza.
l) To finish, sprinkle chopped bell peppers and shaved Parmigiano-Reggiano on top.
m) Preheat your grill or oven to the desired temperature. Place the pizza in the grill or oven. Grill or bake for 16 to 18 minutes. Check the pizza frequently to ensure that the crust is golden and the cheese is melted and bubbly. Once the pizza is ready, remove it from the grill or oven.
n) Remove the Pizza from the heat source and allow it to cool down for a couple of minutes before cutting it into slices.

12) *Philly Cheesesteak Pizza*

Indulge in the mouth-watering fusion of two American classics with our Philly Cheesesteak Pizza. This pizza masterpiece draws inspiration from the iconic Philadelphia sandwich, elevating it to a whole new level of deliciousness. This pizza combines tender and thinly sliced beef, sautéed onions, and melted cheese, capturing the essence of the famous Philly Cheesesteak. Indulge in a delicious medley of toppings atop a sturdy pizza crust that perfectly complements the mouthwatering ingredients. Savor every bite without worrying about the base crumbling under the weight of hearty toppings. Indulge in a mouthwatering experience with every bite of our savory beef, sweet onions, and gooey melted cheese. The combination of flavors and textures will leave your taste buds singing in harmony. Indulge in the savory and satisfying flavors of Philly Cheesesteak Pizza, a delectable dish that pays homage to the culinary traditions of Philadelphia. Whether you're a fan of the classic Philly Cheesesteak or simply seeking a flavorful and indulgent pizza experience, this dish is sure to delight your taste buds.

Makes: 1 Large Pizza
Baking Time: 10-15 minutes

Ingredients:
- 1 recipe Italian Thick Crust Dough
- 1 Onion, sliced
- 8 ounces of Mushrooms, sliced
- ¼ cup of Grated Parmesan cheese
- 3 table spoons Worcestershire sauce
- 8 ounces of Shaved roast beef
- ¼ tea spoon Black pepper
- 1 Green pepper, sliced
- 3 table spoons Olive oil
- 1 tea spoon Crushed garlic
- 4 cups of Provolone cheese

Instructions:
a) Shaved roast beef - Sliced onions - Sliced mushrooms - Olive oil.
b) Heat a skillet over medium-high heat. Add olive oil to the skillet. Add shaved roast beef, sliced onions, and sliced mushrooms to the skillet.
c) Stir-fry for three minutes.
d) In a skillet, incorporate black pepper and Worcestershire sauce.
e) Preheat the oven to the desired temperature. Brush the prepared dough with olive oil. Cover the entire surface of the dough with crushed garlic.
f) Take the dough and spread a thin layer of shredded Provolone cheese on top.
g) I Sauté the roast beef, onions, and mushrooms. Place the cheese on a plate. Evenly distribute the sautéed roast beef, onions, and mushrooms over the cheese.
h) Garnish the dish with grated Parmesan cheese and the remaining shredded Provolone cheese.
i) Preheat oven to 500°F (260°C).
j) Place the pizza in the oven. Bake for 15 minutes. Check the pizza to ensure that the crust is golden and the cheese is melted and bubbly.
k) Remove from the oven. Allow the dish to cool for a few minutes. Then serve and enjoy!

13) *Prosciutto and Arugula Pizza*

Indulge in the delectable fusion of Italian flavors with our Prosciutto and Arugula Pizza. The salty and delicate prosciutto perfectly complements the peppery bite of arugula, creating a truly delightful culinary experience. Indulge in the perfect harmony of flavors with our exquisite pizza that is both elegant and refreshing. Indulge in the delectable thin slices of prosciutto, a dry-cured Italian ham, that bring a savory and slightly salty element to the pizza. Complemented by the vibrant and peppery arugula leaves that lend a fresh and vibrant touch, this pizza is a true masterpiece. Elevate your pizza experience with a final touch of premium olive oil and a generous sprinkle of savory Parmesan cheese, adding depth and richness to every bite. Indulge in the exquisite flavors of Italy with our Prosciutto and Arugula Pizza. This culinary masterpiece embodies the perfect balance of simplicity and sophistication, reminiscent of a classic antipasto platter. Every bite is a delectable journey through the heart of Italian cuisine.

Makes: 1 Large Pizza
Baking Time: 15 minutes

Ingredients:
- 1 recipe for Traditional Italian basic Dough
- 2 ounces of Prosciutto
- ¼ cup of Pizza Sauce
- 1 table spoon Balsamic vinegar
- 3 ounces of Mozzarella cheese, sliced
- ½ cup of Arugula leaves

Instructions:
a) To shape the dough, hold the edges and carefully rotate and stretch it until it forms a 14-inch-diameter circle.
b) Take the pizza dough and place it on a flat surface. - Pour the pizza sauce on top of the dough. - Using a spoon or spatula, spread the pizza sauce evenly across the dough.
c) Evenly distribute the slices of mozzarella cheese on top of the sauce.
d) Take the pizza. Cover it with arugula leaves. Place prosciutto strips on top.
e) Preheat the grill or oven to the highest temperature.
f) Preheat the grill or oven. Place the dish with the pizza in the grill or oven. Grill or bake for 15 minutes. Check if the crust is golden and the cheese is melted and bubbly. Remove from the grill or oven.
g) Allow the pizza to cool down. Drizzle balsamic vinegar over the pizza. Slice and serve the pizza.

14) *Reuben pizza*

Experience the mouthwatering fusion of two classic favorites with Reuben Pizza. This delectable dish pays tribute to the beloved Reuben sandwich by artfully infusing its iconic flavors onto a perfectly baked pizza crust. Experience the unexpected with our one-of-a-kind Reuben pizza. We've taken the classic ingredients of a Reuben sandwich - succulent corned beef, tangy sauerkraut, creamy Swiss cheese, and zesty Thousand Island dressing - and transformed them into a mouthwatering pizza that will leave you craving more. Indulge in the rich and savory flavor of our corned beef, perfectly complemented by the crisp and tangy notes of sauerkraut. Indulge in the rich and velvety goodness of melted Swiss cheese that perfectly envelopes the toppings, creating a comforting and satisfying layer of flavor. Experience the ultimate flavor fusion with our Reuben-inspired pizza. A perfect blend of corned beef, sauerkraut, and melted Swiss cheese, all topped off with a tantalizing drizzle of Thousand Island dressing. It's a taste sensation you won't want to miss. Indulge in the delectable flavors of Reuben Pizza, where classic pizza meets the beloved deli sandwich. This innovative twist on traditional pizza is sure to captivate the taste buds of pizza enthusiasts everywhere.

Makes: 1 Large Pizza
Baking Time: 16-18 minutes

Ingredients:
- 1 recipe for Traditional Italian basic Dough
- 4 ounces of Sliced cooked deli corned beef
- 3 table spoons Deli mustard
- 1 cup of Sauerkraut
- 6 ounces of Shredded Swiss, Emmental, Jarlsberg, or Jarlsberg Cheese

Instructions:
a) To shape the dough, hold the edges and carefully rotate and stretch it until it forms a 14-inch-diameter circle.
b) Take the pizza dough and place it on a flat surface. - Pour the pizza sauce on top of the dough. - Using a spoon or spatula, spread the pizza sauce evenly across the dough.
c) Evenly distribute the slices of mozzarella cheese on top of the sauce.
d) Take the pizza. Cover it with arugula leaves. Place prosciutto strips on top.
e) Preheat the grill or oven to the highest temperature.
f) Preheat the grill or oven. Place the dish with the pizza in the grill or oven. Grill or bake for 15 minutes. Check if the crust is golden and the cheese is melted and bubbly. Remove from the grill or oven.
g) Allow the pizza to cool down. Drizzle balsamic vinegar over the pizza. Slice and serve the pizza.

15) *Pizza for Easter*

Celebrate this joyous holiday with a delicious and versatile option - Pizza for Easter! Indulge in the ultimate dining experience with pizza, the perfect addition to any festive gathering. Whether it's a brunch, lunch, or dinner, this versatile dish offers endless possibilities for customization, making it a crowd-pleaser for all ages. Celebrate the season of renewal with Easter-themed pizzas featuring a variety of delectable toppings. From savory ham to fresh asparagus and artichokes, or even colorful vegetables, the possibilities are endless. Indulge in your personal preference for crust - whether it's thin and crispy or thick and fluffy. Celebrate Easter with a delicious and satisfying meal that brings loved ones together. Pizza is the perfect choice to foster a sense of togetherness and joy during this special holiday. Elevate your Easter dining experience with the comforting and versatile addition of pizza. Whether it's the centerpiece of your meal or a fun and casual option for festivities, pizza is sure to delight.

Makes: 1 Pizza
Baking Time: 50-60 minutes

Ingredients:

- ⅔ pounds Frozen bread dough, thawed
- ½ pounds Italian sausage, cooked
- ½ pounds Mozzarella, sliced
- 16 ounces of Ricotta cheese
- ½ cup of Grated Parmesan cheese
- ½ pounds Sliced provolone cheese
- ½ pounds Sliced salami
- ½ pounds Sliced cooked ham
- ½ pounds Sliced pepperoni
- 8 eggs, beaten
- Olive oil
- 1 egg
- 1 tea spoon water

Instructions:

a) Take the thawed bread dough and layer it in a springform pan.
b) Spread the pizza crust onto a baking sheet. Add the toppings in the following order: Italian sausage, mozzarella, ricotta cheese, Parmesan cheese, provolone cheese, salami, cooked ham, and pepperoni. Repeat step 2 with the remaining half of toppings. Bake the pizza according to the crust instructions.
c) Layer the ingredients as instructed in the previous step. - Repeat the layering process.
d) Roll out a 12-inch pizza dough. Place the dough on top of the pizza to form the top crust.
e) In a mixing bowl, combine 1 egg and water. Whisk until well blended. Brush the top of the pizza with the egg wash.
f) To bake the pizza, preheat the oven to 350 degrees Fahrenheit (175 degrees Celsius). Place the pizza in the oven and bake for 50 to 60 minutes.

16) *Flatbread Pizza*

Experience a lighter and more rustic twist on the classic pizza with Flatbread Pizza. Indulge in the delectable taste of our pizza with its thin and crispy crust that perfectly complements the flavors of the toppings, making each bite a truly delightful experience. Experience a world of culinary possibilities with the versatile flatbread. Elevate your taste buds with classic Margherita, featuring fresh tomatoes and basil, or indulge in more daring options like fig and goat cheese or prosciutto and arugula. Indulge in a lighter and more delicate pizza experience with Flatbread Pizza. Savor the delicious taste and variety without any compromise. Indulge in the simplicity and versatility of flatbread pizza, perfect for any occasion. Whether as an appetizer, light meal, or party snack, this culinary creation is sure to delight your taste buds.

Makes: 1 Large Pizza
Baking Time: about 10 minutes

Ingredients:
- 1 prepared 12-inch flatbread crust
- 6 sliced crimini mushrooms
- 1 and a half pounds smoked bacon
- 6 cups of grated asiago cheese
- 3 chopped garlic cloves
- Pinch of salt and black pepper
- 8 spears of trimmed and cut-up asparagus
- 3 cups of marinara sauce
- 2 tablespoons olive oil
- 6 cups of grated mozzarella cheese

Instructions:
a) Pan-fry the mushrooms in oil with garlic, salt, and black pepper.
b) In a separate pan, cook the asparagus for about 8 minutes.
c) Cook the bacon for about 10 minutes in the same skillet, then transfer it to a plate lined with paper towels to drain.
d) Evenly distribute the flatbread crust on a sheet pan.
e) Spread marinara sauce over the crust before adding bacon, asparagus, mushrooms, mozzarella cheese, and grated asiago cheese.
f) Bake for 12 to 15 minutes.

17) *Hamburger Pizza*

Indulge in the ultimate comfort food experience with Hamburger Pizza, a delicious fusion of two beloved classics—the iconic hamburger and the timeless pizza. Indulge in a mouth-watering pizza experience with our latest creation. Our star ingredient, a juicy beef patty, is perfectly complemented by classic burger toppings like melted cheese, crisp lettuce, juicy tomatoes, and tangy pickles. Experience the perfect combination of texture and flavor with our crust that doubles as a sturdy bun, providing a reliable foundation for your hearty toppings. Indulge in the mouthwatering blend of savory beef, gooey melted cheese, and the classic taste of a juicy hamburger with every single bite. Experience the ultimate fusion of two classic favorites with Hamburger Pizza. This deliciously indulgent creation is sure to satisfy your cravings for both pizza and burgers in one mouthwatering bite.

Makes: 1 Large Pizza
Baking Time: about 10 minutes

Ingredients:

- 8 hamburger buns, split
- 2 and a quarter teaspoons Italian seasoning
- 1 teaspoon garlic powder
- ⅛ teaspoon red pepper flakes
- ⅓ cup of chopped onion

- ⅓ cup of grated Parmesan cheese
- 1 pound ground beef
- ¼ teaspoon onion powder
- 1 teaspoon paprika
- 15 ounces of pizza sauce
- 2 cups of shredded mozzarella cheese

Instructions:

a) Broil the bun halves for about a minute.
b) To cook the ground beef, place it in a skillet and simmer for 10 minutes or until fully cooked.
c) Incorporate the chopped onion into the mixture and stir-fry for an extra 5 minutes.
d) In a skillet, add Italian seasoning, garlic powder, red pepper flakes, grated Parmesan cheese, onion powder, and paprika. Pour pizza sauce into the skillet. Mix all ingredients together. Simmer the mixture for 10 to 15 minutes.
e) Preheat the oven to 375°F. Place the bun halves on a sheet pan. Spread the beef mixture evenly on top of the bun halves. Sprinkle shredded mozzarella cheese on top of the beef mixture. Place the sheet pan in the preheated oven and bake for 10-12 minutes or until the cheese is melted and bubbly. Remove from the oven and serve hot.

18) *Breakfast Pizza*

Indulge in the mouthwatering combination of breakfast and pizza with our Breakfast Pizza. Start your day off right with a hearty and satisfying meal that will tantalize your taste buds. Indulge in a breakfast-inspired pizza with a delectable biscuit or hash brown crust, topped with classic morning staples such as fluffy scrambled eggs, crispy bacon or sausage, and gooey melted cheese. Indulge in the delightful harmony of savory and indulgent flavors that are sure to appeal to breakfast lovers. Indulge in the ultimate breakfast experience with our mouth-watering Breakfast Pizza. This versatile dish allows you to customize it with your favorite toppings such as fresh vegetables, aromatic herbs, or a spicy drizzle of hot sauce. With endless possibilities to suit your unique taste and preferences, Breakfast Pizza is the perfect way to start your day. Indulge in the perfect blend of breakfast and pizza with our Breakfast Pizza. Savor the comforting flavors of a hearty breakfast, whether you're looking for a weekend brunch treat or a quick and convenient breakfast option.

Makes: 1 Large Pizza
Baking Time: 20-25 minutes

Ingredients:
- 1 traditional pizza dough
- 6 eggs, beaten
- Half a cup of sliced green onion
- Half a cup of pizza sauce
- Salt and pepper
- ¼ cup of grated Parmesan cheese
- 6 slices chopped bacon
- 2 ounces of sliced salami

Instructions:
a) Heat a skillet over medium-high heat. Add bacon to the skillet and cook until well browned.
b) Heat a wok or large skillet over high heat. Add the green onions to the wok or skillet. Stir-fry the green onions for approximately 1 minute.
c) Crack the eggs into a bowl. Add salt and pepper to taste. Whisk the eggs until fully scrambled.
d) Spread the pizza sauce evenly over the dough.
e) Sprinkle grated Parmesan cheese on top. Add chopped bacon. Place sliced salami on top. Add scrambled eggs on top.
f) Preheat the oven to 400 degrees Fahrenheit (200 degrees Celsius). Place the dish in the oven and bake for 20 to 25 minutes.

19) *Grilled White Pizza with Soppressata*

Elevate your pizza game with our Grilled White Pizza featuring savory Soppressata and a tantalizing blend of smoky and charred flavors. Indulge in a one-of-a-kind pizza experience with our signature variation. Our expertly crafted dough boasts a perfect balance of chewiness and softness, complemented by a delectable blend of olive oil and garlic that serves as the foundation for a truly unforgettable flavor journey. Indulge in the rich and velvety white sauce, crafted with a delectable combination of ricotta, mozzarella, and Parmesan cheese, instead of the usual tomato sauce. Indulge in our mouth-watering pizza, crowned with delicate slices of soppressata - a dry-cured Italian salami that boasts a rich and subtly spicy taste. Elevate your pizza game by grilling it to perfection, adding a smoky and charred element that enhances the depth of flavors. Indulge in a truly exquisite and refined pizza experience that caters to the palates of cheese and charcuterie aficionados alike.

Makes: 1 Large Pizza
Baking Time: 10-17 minutes

Ingredients:
- 1 traditional pizza dough
- 1 tea spoon chopped thyme
- 1 cup of whole milk ricotta
- 2 tea spoons oregano
- 1 table spoon garlic-infused olive oil
- 4 cups of shredded mozzarella
- 1 cup of grated Parmesan
- 6 ounces of sliced Soppressata
- 4 ounces of drained and torn cherry peppers

Instructions:
a) On a lightly floured surface, spread out the dough.
b) Gently roll or stretch out the dough into a circle.
c) Layer the dough with ricotta, oregano, and chopped thyme.
d) To assemble the pizza, begin by spreading garlic-infused olive oil over the dough. Next, add a layer of mozzarella cheese, followed by Parmesan cheese, Soppressata, and cherry peppers.
e) Cook the pizza for 5 to 10 minutes on each side.

20) *Muffuletta Pizza*

Experience the mouthwatering fusion of two iconic dishes with Muffuletta Pizza. This delectable creation pays tribute to the beloved New Orleans sandwich, the muffuletta, and elevates it to a whole new level of deliciousness. Experience the ultimate pizza indulgence with our one-of-a-kind creation. Our signature crust is elevated with a delectable layer of olive salad, boasting a harmonious blend of savory olives, tangy pickled vegetables, and fragrant Italian herbs. Indulge in a mouthwatering assortment of cured Italian meats, including savory salami, succulent ham, and delectable mortadella, all resting atop a bed of fresh olive salad. Complementing this savory blend is a generous serving of sliced provolone cheese. Experience the spirit of the Large Easy with our mouthwatering sandwich. The briny and tangy olive salad perfectly complements the richness of the meats, while the creamy provolone cheese adds a touch of indulgence. It's a symphony of flavors that will leave your taste buds singing. Orleans in every bite. Experience a unique

Makes: 3 Pizzas
Baking Time: 8-10 minutes

Ingredients:
- 2 12" uncooked pizza dough crusts
- 3 table spoons extra virgin olive oil
- ¼ cup of chopped pepperoncini
- 2 tea spoons Italian salad dressing mix
- 8 ounces of shredded provolone cheese
- ¼ cup of chopped onions
- ½ cup of chopped celery
- 1 clove garlic, chopped
- 3 ounces of diced deli ham/salami
- ⅓ cup of chopped pimento-stuffed green olives

Instructions:
a) Combine all toppings in a mixing bowl, excluding the olive oil.
b) Evenly distribute the topping mixture onto a single pizza dough crust.
c) Instructions for preparing the topping: Coat the topping with a light layer of olive oil.
d) Preheat your oven to 500°F. Preheat the oven to the desired temperature. Place the pizza on a baking sheet or directly on the oven rack. Bake for 8 to 10 minutes or until the crust is golden brown and the cheese is melted.

21) *Dutch oven pizza*

Experience the ultimate joy of pizza-making in the great outdoors with Dutch Oven Pizza. Experience the perfect pizza with our cast-iron Dutch oven cooking style. Enjoy an evenly cooked pizza with a crispy crust that will leave you craving for more. Experience the rustic and delicious taste of Dutch Oven Pizza whether you're camping, enjoying a backyard barbecue, or simply looking to try a unique cooking method. Indulge in a wide variety of toppings that cater to all palates, from the timeless pepperoni and mozzarella to the more daring blends of crisp veggies and artisanal cheeses. Experience the rustic allure and delectable taste of Dutch Oven Pizza, as you relish in the pleasures of outdoor cooking and indulge in a slice of pizza amidst the beauty of nature.

Makes: 1 Large Pizza
Baking Time: 30 minutes

Ingredients:
- 2 packages of crescent rolls
- 1 jar of pizza sauce
- 1.5 pounds ground beef
- 8 ounces of grated cheddar cheese
- 8 ounces of grated mozzarella cheese
- 4 ounces of pepperoni
- 2 tea spoons oregano
- 1 tea spoon garlic powder
- 1 tea spoon onion powder

Instructions:
a) Heat a pan over medium-high heat. - Add the ground beef and cook until browned. - Drain the fat from the pan.
b) Take one package of crescent rolls. - Line a Dutch oven with the crescent rolls.
c) Spread the pizza sauce evenly over the dough.
d) Spread the pizza dough on a baking sheet. Add tomato sauce on top of the dough. Sprinkle oregano, garlic powder, and onion powder on top of the tomato sauce. Add pepperoni and ground beef on top of the spices.
e) To prepare the top crust, take the second package of crescent rolls and layer them over the cheese.
f) Preheat the oven to the desired temperature. Place the pizza in the oven. Bake for 30 minutes.

22) *Hot Italian Skillet Pizza*

Experience the fiery and flavorful taste of Hot Italian Skillet Pizza! This pizza variation pays tribute to the bold and spicy flavors of Italian cuisine, making it a must-try for any foodie looking for a delicious and exciting meal. Indulge in the irresistible taste of our pizza, expertly crafted to perfection in a sizzling hot skillet. The result? A mouth-watering, crispy crust with a golden hue that will leave you craving for more. Indulge in our mouth-watering toppings, including zesty Italian sausage, savory peppers, and onions, all perfectly seasoned with a generous sprinkle of crushed red pepper flakes for an added burst of flavor. Experience the perfect balance of heat from the sausage and spices, harmoniously blended with the gooey melted cheese, resulting in a truly delectable flavor. Indulge in the fiery and lively taste of Hot Italian Skillet Pizza, perfect for those who crave a daring and zesty pizza adventure.

Makes: 1 Large Pizza
Baking Time: 5-10 minutes

Ingredients:
- 1 table spoon olive oil
- 1 onion, sliced
- 1 green bell pepper, sliced
- 3.5 ounces of sliced Italian sausage
- ¼ cup of sliced fresh mushrooms
- 1 slice polenta
- ¼ cup of spaghetti sauce
- 1 ounce shredded mozzarella cheese

Instructions:
a) To cook the sausage, onion, bell pepper, and mushrooms, heat olive oil in a skillet. Cook for 10 to 15 minutes.
b) Heat a skillet over medium-high heat. Place the polenta in the skillet. Cook for approximately 5 minutes on each side.
c) Place the sausage mixture on top of the polenta, then add spaghetti sauce and mozzarella cheese.
d) Bake the pizza for 5 to 10 minutes.

23) *Lorraine Pizza*

Experience the mouthwatering fusion of French and Italian cuisine with Lorraine Pizza. Inspired by the iconic Quiche Lorraine, this pizza creation is a delicious twist on a classic dish. Indulge in the ultimate pizza experience with our one-of-a-kind creation. Our signature flaky and buttery crust is perfectly complemented by a delectable blend of creamy eggs, savory cheese, crispy bacon, and flavorful onions. Experience a symphony of flavors with our delectable dish featuring smoky bacon, rich cheese, and a delicate custard-like texture of the egg mixture. Experience the perfect blend of French and Italian culinary traditions with Lorraine Pizza. Our innovative flavor combinations showcase the versatility and creativity that can be achieved with pizza as a canvas.

Makes: 1 Large Pizza
Baking Time: 16 to 18 minutes

Ingredients:

- 1 recipe for Traditional Italian basic Dough
- 5 ounces of diced bacon
- 1 table spoon heavy cream
- 2 tea spoons stemmed thyme leaves
- 8 ounces of shredded Swiss, Emmental, Gruyère, or Muenster cheese
- ¼ cup of diced red onion
- 1 egg

Instructions:

a) Prepare the traditional Italian basic dough recipe and shape it into a 14-inch-diameter circle by gently stretching and rotating the dough.

b) Cook the diced bacon in a skillet until it becomes soft and starts to brown.

c) In a bowl, combine the beaten egg and heavy cream until thick and creamy.

d) Spread the egg and cream mixture evenly over the dough.

e) Sprinkle the shredded Swiss, Emmental, Gruyère, or Muenster cheese on top of the cream mixture, followed by the cooked bacon, diced red onion, and stemmed thyme leaves.

f) Grill or bake the pizza at the appropriate temperature for 16 to 18 minutes, or until the crust is golden and the cheese has melted.

g) Allow the pizza to cool for about five minutes before slicing and serving.

24) *Picadillo Pizza*

Experience the bold and exciting flavors of Latin America in a whole new way with Picadillo Pizza. Our unique blend of ingredients will take your taste buds on a journey like never before. Experience the bold and savory flavors of Latin America with our Picadillo Pizza. Our expertly crafted pizza is topped with a delicious blend of seasoned ground meat, juicy tomatoes, aromatic onions, and a tantalizing mix of spices and herbs. Savor every bite of this mouthwatering dish that's sure to satisfy your cravings. Indulge in the perfect combination of a sturdy crust and robust picadillo, topped off with melted cheese for a creamy and comforting experience. Indulge in a one-of-a-kind culinary adventure with Picadillo Pizza's fusion of Latin American and Italian flavors. Our expertly crafted pies are a delicious and culturally rich experience that will leave your taste buds wanting more.

Makes: 1 Large Pizza
Baking Time: 16 to 18 minutes

Ingredients:

- 1 recipe for Traditional Italian basic Dough
- 4 garlic cloves, chopped
- Pickled jalapeño slices
- 1 plum tomato, chopped
- ½ teaspoon cracked black pepper
- 6 ounces of shredded Manchego cheese
- 1 teaspoon dried oregano
- 1 hard-cooked egg, chopped

- 1 scallion, chopped
- 1 tablespoon of olive oil
- 5 tablespoons of chopped parsley leaves
- ¼ cup chopped, pitted green olives
- 2 tablespoons of chopped golden raisins
- 2 teaspoons Worcestershire sauce
- ½ pound of lean ground beef
- ½ teaspoon salt

Instructions:

a) Prepare the traditional Italian basic dough recipe and shape it into a 14-inch-diameter circle by gently stretching and rotating the dough.
b) In a skillet, heat olive oil over medium heat and cook the chopped garlic for about 30 seconds.
c) Add the ground beef to the skillet and cook, stirring often, for 4 to 5 minutes or until it is well-browned.
d) Stir in the chopped tomato, hard-cooked egg, scallion, olives, raisins, dried oregano, Worcestershire sauce, salt, black pepper, and chopped jalapeños.
e) Sprinkle the shredded Manchego cheese over the dough.
f) Spoon the cooked ground beef mixture evenly on top.
g) Cook or grill the pizza at the appropriate temperature for 16 to 18 minutes, or until the crust is golden and the cheese has melted.
h) Garnish with the remaining chopped parsley.

25) *Worcestershire Pizza*

Experience the bold and irresistible taste of Worcestershire sauce with our Worcestershire Pizza. Each bite is bursting with tangy and savory flavors that will leave your taste buds craving for more. Indulge in a pizza like no other with our latest creation. Our signature crust is brushed with Worcestershire sauce, delivering a bold and distinctive flavor that is sure to tantalize your taste buds. Indulge in a mouth-watering medley of toppings that can vary, but are sure to include savory grilled steak, delectable caramelized onions, and a tantalizing blend of cheeses. Experience the mouthwatering blend of tangy and savory flavors with our pizza infused with Worcestershire sauce. The unique umami taste of this sauce adds a depth of flavor that will leave your taste buds wanting more. Experience a tantalizing twist on traditional pizza with Worcestershire Pizza. Our unique take showcases the versatility of this beloved condiment in the realm of pizza-making.

Makes: 3
Baking Time: 15-20 minutes

Ingredients:

- 10 ounces of chilled biscuit dough
- 1¼ cups of pizza sauce
- 1 cup of shredded mozzarella cheese
- ½ pound of lean ground beef
- ½ teaspoon Worcestershire sauce
- 1 cup of diced pepperoni
- 1 cup of feta cheese crumbles
- 1 egg yolk
- ½ teaspoon hot pepper sauce
- Salt and black pepper to taste

Instructions:

a) Grease a cookie sheet or line it with parchment paper.
b) In a pan, cook the lean ground beef until it is well browned.
c) Add Worcestershire sauce, hot pepper sauce, diced pepperoni, feta cheese crumbles, salt, and black pepper to the cooked ground beef. Stir to combine the ingredients.
d) Preheat the oven to 375°F (190°C).
e) On a lightly floured surface, roll out the chilled biscuit dough to about 1/4-inch thickness.
f) Use a round object, such as the bottom of a glass, to cut the dough into 5-inch-diameter circles.
g) In a small bowl, whisk the egg yolk with 1/4 teaspoon of water to make an egg wash.
h) Place the biscuit circles on the prepared cookie sheet. Brush the dough with the egg wash.
i) Spoon a portion of the beef mixture onto the center of each biscuit circle, leaving a small border around the edges.
j) Top each biscuit with a generous amount of pizza sauce and sprinkle shredded mozzarella cheese on top.
k) Bake in the preheated oven for 15 to 20 minutes, or until the biscuits are golden brown and the cheese is melted and bubbly.
l) Remove from the oven and let cool slightly before serving.

26) *Backroad Pizza*

Experience the thrill of discovery with Backroad Pizza, where every bite is a voyage into uncharted flavor territory. Our menu beckons you to venture beyond the ordinary and embrace the unexpected. Come join us on a culinary expedition off the beaten path. Discover the rustic charm of this pizza style, commonly found in quaint pizzerias and food trucks nestled along scenic backroads and country lanes. Experience the essence of the region with our pizza toppings that are crafted to showcase the local and seasonal ingredients. Experience the true taste of locally sourced and thoughtfully crafted ingredients with Backroad Pizza. From farm-fresh produce to artisanal cheeses and homemade sauces, our menu captures the essence of quality and flavor. Experience the perfect pizza crust, tailored to your liking. Our pizzerias offer a variety of styles, from thin and crispy to thick and chewy. Indulge in a mouth-watering and genuine culinary adventure with Backroad Pizza. Our offerings are sure to uncover hidden gems and inspire you to embrace the thrill of venturing off the beaten path.

Makes: 1 Large Pizza
Baking Time: 15 minutes

Ingredients:
- 8 ounces of shredded Cheddar cheese
- 1 tomato, sliced
- 1 pound ground beef
- 10¾ ounces of condensed cream of mushroom soup

Instructions:
a) Preheat the oven to 425 degrees Fahrenheit.
b) In a skillet, pan-fry the ground beef until thoroughly cooked.
c) Spread the condensed cream of mushroom soup over the pizza crust.
d) Arrange the tomato slices on top of the cheese and cooked beef.
e) Bake for approximately 15 minutes.

27) *Pennsylvanian Style Pizza*

Discover the unique and delicious Pennsylvanian Style Pizza, a regional pizza variation that hails from the great state of Pennsylvania in the United States. Indulge in the delectable goodness of our signature style, featuring a thick and doughy crust that is perfectly complemented by a sweet and tangy tomato sauce and an abundance of melted cheese. Indulge in the robust flavors of our toppings atop a sturdy and chewy crust that provides the perfect foundation for a truly satisfying pizza experience. Indulge in a variety of toppings ranging from classic choices like pepperoni, sausage, and mushrooms to regional favorites like sweet peppers or scrapple, a Pennsylvania Dutch delicacy. Indulge in the one-of-a-kind Pennsylvanian Style Pizza that puts a regional spin on the classic pie. Savor the rich culinary heritage and distinct flavors of the Keystone State with every bite.

Makes: 1 Large Pizza
Baking Time: about 10 minutes

Ingredients:
- 1-pound whole wheat dough
- 1 cup of rinsed and drained sauerkraut
- ½ cup of Thousand Island dressing
- ½ tea spoon caraway seeds
- 2 cups of shredded Swiss cheese
- 6 ounces of deli-sliced corned beef
- ¼ cup of chopped dill pickles

Instructions:
a) Grease a pizza pan and preheat the oven to 375 degrees Fahrenheit.
b) Roll out the bread dough on a floured surface into a 14-inch diameter circle.
c) Transfer the dough to the pizza pan and seal the edges.
d) Bake the crust for 20 to 25 minutes.
e) Remove the crust from the oven and evenly spread half of the salad dressing over it.
f) Layer half of the Swiss cheese, corned beef, remaining salad dressing, sauerkraut, and the remaining half of the Swiss cheese.
g) Sprinkle the caraway seeds evenly on top.
h) Bake for approximately 10 minutes.
i) Serve garnished with pickle slices.

28) *Mexican Pizza*

Experience the perfect fusion of Mexican cuisine and pizza with our mouth-watering Mexican Pizza. Savor the vibrant and bold flavors of Mexico in every bite, while enjoying the comfort of a classic pizza. Indulge in the ultimate fusion of flavors with our signature dish. A crispy tortilla or tortilla-like crust serves as the perfect foundation for a mouthwatering medley of seasoned ground beef, refried beans, zesty salsa, and gooey cheese. Topped off with a vibrant array of colorful veggies like juicy tomatoes, zesty onions, and spicy jalapeños, this dish is sure to tantalize your taste buds. Indulge in a mouthwatering culinary experience with the perfect combination of savory and spicy flavors, complemented by the satisfying crunch of a tortilla crust. Experience a burst of flavor with Mexican Pizza - a unique twist on the classic pizza that brings the vibrant and festive tastes of Mexico to your taste buds. Satisfy your cravings and indulge in this delicious fusion of two beloved cuisines.

Makes: 4 pizzas
Baking Time: 8-12 minutes

Ingredients:

- 8 flour tortillas
- 1 cup of shortening or cooking oil
- ½ tea spoon salt
- ⅔ cup of picante salsa
- ¼ tea spoon chopped onion
- 16 ounces of canned refried beans
- ½ pound ground beef
- ¼ tea spoon paprika

- 1½ tea spoons chili powder
- ¼ cup of sliced black olives
- 1 cup of grated Cheddar cheese
- 2 table spoons water
- ⅓ cup of diced tomato
- 1 cup of grated Monterey Jack cheese
- ¼ cup of chopped green onions

Instructions:

a) Preheat the oven to 400°F.
b) In a skillet, cook the ground beef over medium-low heat.
c) Season the ground beef with salt, chopped onion, paprika, chili powder, and water. Simmer until cooked through.
d) In a separate frying pan, fry the tortillas in hot oil or shortening for 45 seconds.
e) Heat the refried beans in a pan.
f) Spread about a third of the refried beans onto one tortilla.
g) Layer the cooked ground beef on top of the beans, followed by another tortilla.
h) Spread 2 table spoons of salsa over each pizza and top with diced tomatoes.
i) Arrange the Cheddar cheese, green onions, and black olives evenly.
j) Bake the pizzas for 8 to 12 minutes.

CHAPTER 3: POULTRY PIZZA

29) *Pizza with Italian Buffalo Chicken*

Experience the ultimate flavor sensation with our Italian Buffalo Chicken Pizza. Savor the bold and tangy taste of buffalo chicken perfectly paired with the comforting goodness of pizza. Indulge in our mouth-watering pizza variation, boasting succulent and fiery chicken, marinated to perfection in a tangy buffalo sauce. The chicken is perfectly paired with a delectable blend of Italian cheeses, including the creamy mozzarella and the bold gorgonzola. Experience a burst of flavors and textures with our spicy chicken, creamy and tangy cheeses, and crispy crust. It's a delightful combination that will leave your taste buds wanting more. Indulge in the ultimate flavor experience with our Italian Buffalo Chicken Pizza. This mouth-watering creation puts a delicious spin on the classic buffalo chicken and traditional pizza, delivering a spicy and satisfying meal that will leave your taste buds begging for more.

Makes: 1 Large Pizza
Baking Time: 10-15 minutes

Ingredients:
- One traditional Italian basic dough recipe
- 1 teaspoon each of unsalted butter and Worcestershire sauce
- Three ounces of grated mozzarella
- 2 oz. of blue cheese
- 10 ounces of sliced boneless, skinless chicken breasts and 3 ounces of shredded Monterey Jack
- 3 sliced celery ribs
- 1 teaspoon of red pepper sauce
- Six tablespoons of chili sauce

Instructions:
a) A 14-inch-diameter circle should be formed out of the dough by carefully turning and stretching it while holding the edges.
b) Melt the butter in a skillet or wok.
c) In the skillet, cook the chicken slices for 5 minutes.
d) Before turning off the heat, drizzle Worcestershire sauce and hot red pepper sauce over the cooked chicken.
e) Cover the dough with the chili sauce and cooked chicken.
f) Distribute the celery slices, mozzarella, and monterey jack cheese evenly on the pizza.
g) Finally, sprinkle blue cheese crumbles over the other toppings in a uniform layer.
h) 15 minutes or so in the oven.

30) *Pizza with duck confit and smoked kielbasa*

Elevate your pizza experience with our Duck Confit and Smoked Kielbasa Pizza. Savor the rich and savory flavors that come together in this indulgent masterpiece. Indulge in a one-of-a-kind pizza experience with our exquisite duck confit, a French culinary delicacy, paired with slices of smoky kielbasa sausage. Savor the tender and flavorful combination that will leave your taste buds wanting more. Indulge in a delectable blend of toppings perfectly paired with a rich and velvety fusion of cheeses, such as fontina or Gruyère, that will melt in your mouth. Indulge in a pizza experience that is both refined and comforting. Our expertly crafted pie boasts a harmonious fusion of textures and flavors that will tantalize even the most daring taste buds. Indulge in the ultimate gourmet experience with our Pizza featuring succulent Duck Confit and savory Smoked Kielbasa. This unique twist on traditional pizza brings together the sophistication of French cuisine and the robust flavors of smoked sausage, creating a truly irresistible combination that will tantalize your taste buds.

Makes: 1 Large Pizza
Baking Time: 16 to 18 minutes

Ingredients:
- One traditional Italian basic dough recipe
- 1 head of roasted garlic
- 2 table spoons of chopped sage leaves
- 2 tea spoons of stemmed thyme leaves
- ½ tea spoon of salt
- ⅓ cup of canned white beans, drained and rinsed
- ½ tea spoon of cracked black pepper
- 2 ounces of smoked kielbasa
- 1 fried egg (optional)
- 4 ounces of shredded Gruyère
- 4 ounces of shredded duck confit legs
- 1½ ounces of Grated Parmigiana

Instructions:
a) A 14-inch-diameter circle should be formed out of the dough by carefully turning and stretching it while holding the edges.
b) Scatter grated Gruyère over the crust.
c) Arrange the white beans and cheese on the pizza, followed by squeezing the roasted garlic pulp over top.
d) Season the pizza with salt, pepper, sage, and thyme.
e) Spread the shredded duck confit and smoked kielbasa over the pie, then top with grated Parmigiano.
f) Grill the pizza for 16 to 18 minutes or bake it.
g) You can optionally top the dish with a fried egg before serving.

31) *BBQ Chicken Pizza*

Experience the perfect blend of smoky and tangy flavors with our BBQ Chicken Pizza. It's the ultimate combination of barbecue and pizza, taking your taste buds on a delicious journey. Indulge in our mouth-watering pizza variation, boasting tender and juicy chicken cooked to perfection in a flavorful barbecue sauce. The sweet and savory element of this pizza will tantalize your taste buds and leave you craving for more. Indulge in the delectable chicken dish, perfectly paired with a blend of mouth-watering cheeses like mozzarella or cheddar. The addition of savory toppings like red onions and cilantro elevates the overall flavor profile, leaving your taste buds craving for more. Indulge in the ultimate pizza experience with a mouthwatering blend of tanginess, smokiness, and cheesiness that will leave you feeling comforted and satisfied. Indulge in the perfect fusion of two beloved cuisines with our BBQ Chicken Pizza. Savor the mouthwatering flavors of barbecue and pizza coming together in a delightful and crowd-pleasing combination.

Makes: 1 Large Pizza
Baking Time: 15-20 minutes

Ingredients:
- 3 cooked and cubed boneless chicken breast halves
- 1 cup of shredded smoked Gouda cheese
- 1 pre-baked 12-inch pizza crust
- A single cup of barbecue sauce
- 1 tea spoon molasses
- 1 table spoon honey
- 1 bunch cilantro
- 1 cup of sliced red onion

Instructions:
a) The chicken should be cooked with molasses, brown sugar, barbecue sauce, honey, and cilantro in a skillet with hot oil.
b) Top the pre-baked pizza dough with the cooked chicken mixture, shredded smoked Gouda cheese, and thinly sliced red onions
c) Bake the pizza for 15 to 20 minutes at 425 degrees Fahrenheit.

32) *Spicy Spinach Chicken Pizza*

Indulge in the mouthwatering Spicy Spinach Chicken Pizza, where bold flavors and nutritious ingredients come together in perfect harmony. Indulge in a mouthwatering pizza experience with our delectable variation, boasting succulent chicken, sautéed spinach, and a fiery kick of spice from premium ingredients like crushed red pepper flakes or jalapeños. Indulge in the protein-packed goodness of chicken and the fresh, vibrant touch of spinach. Indulge in a mouthwatering blend of spices and flavors that ignite your taste buds with a tantalizing heat. The creamy and melty cheese perfectly balances the flavors, creating a harmonious and satisfying taste experience that will leave you craving for more. Indulge in the delectable Spicy Spinach Chicken Pizza, a wholesome and flavorful option that's loaded with nutritious ingredients.

Makes: 1 Large Pizza
Baking Time: 10-15 minutes

Ingredients:
- 1 piece of Classic Italian Basic Dough
- 6 table spoons of butter
- 6 fried bacon slices
- ½ cup of freshly grated Romano cheese
- 2 minced garlic cloves
- 1 pinch each of nutmeg, paprika, cayenne, cumin, thyme, salt, pepper, and onion powder.
- 2 egg yolks
- 1 tablespoon of vegetable oil
- ½ cup of grated Parmesan cheese
- 1½ cups of heavy cream
- 2 skinless, boneless chicken breast halves
- 1 cup of diced Roma tomato
- ½ cup of baby spinach leaves
- 1 cup of shredded Mozzarella cheese

Instructions:
a) In a skillet, melt the butter and sauté the minced garlic for about a minute.
b) Pour heavy cream and egg yolks into the skillet.
c) Add roughly a half-cup each of Romano and Parmesan cheese, salt, and nutmeg, and simmer for three to five minutes.
d) Combine the cayenne, salt, white pepper, thyme, cumin, paprika, onion powder, and paprika.
e) Evenly cover each chicken breast with the spice mixture on both sides.
f) In 1 teaspoon of vegetable oil, sear the chicken breasts for about a minute on each side.
g) Remove the chicken from the oven after 5 to 10 minutes and slice it.
h) After punching down the pizza dough, roll it out on a floured surface.
i) Poke a few holes in the crust with a fork and bake for 5 to 7 minutes.
j) After taking the crust out of the oven, cover it with three tablespoons of Parmesan cheese and layer on the sliced chicken, baby spinach leaves, bacon, and Alfredo sauce.
k) Bake the pizza for a further 20 minutes at 350°F.
l) Add chopped Roma tomatoes as a garnish.

33) *Pizza Pot Pie*

Experience the ultimate comfort food with Pizza Pot Pie. This hearty dish takes the classic pizza to a whole new level, providing a satisfying and delicious meal that will leave you feeling warm and content. Indulge in a one-of-a-kind pizza experience with our signature deep-dish crust, generously filled with classic pizza fixings like savory sauce, gooey cheese, and your favorite toppings. Experience the ultimate in savory satisfaction with our signature double-layered crust, baked to perfection until it boasts a mouthwatering golden hue and a satisfying crunch. Experience the ultimate comfort food with our pizza pot pie. As you slice open the golden crust, you'll be greeted with a mouthwatering and bubbling filling that will transport you to the nostalgic flavors of a classic pot pie. Indulge in the delectable blend of a luscious sauce, gooey cheese, and robust toppings that culminate in a truly gratifying and comforting taste experience. Experience a new take on pizza with Pizza Pot Pie! Our delicious twist on the classic pizza is sure to satisfy your cravings for something warm and comforting. Indulge in a more substantial pizza experience with Pizza Pot Pie.

Makes: 1 Large Pizza
Baking Time: about 18 minutes

Ingredients:
- One traditional Italian basic dough recipe
- ½ table spoons of unsalted butter
- 1 table spoon of all-purpose flour, and 2 cups of mixed veggies
- 3 dashes of strong red pepper sauce
- a half tea spoon of salt
- 1 cup milk
- 1 cup of chopped, skinned, and cooked chicken
- ½ tea spoon of freshly cracked black pepper
- ½ tea spoons of stemmed thyme leaves
- 1 tea spoon of chopped sage leaves
- 2 tea spoons of Worcestershire sauce
- 6 ounces of shredded Gouda cheese
- 1 tablespoon of Dijon mustard

Instructions:
a) A 14-inch-diameter circle should be formed out of the dough by carefully turning and stretching it while holding the edges.
b) Melt 12 tablespoons of butter in a pan and stir in the flour until it turns pale beige.
c) While whisking, gradually pour the milk into the pan.
d) Include the mustard, chopped sage leaves, and thyme leaves in the pan.
e) Turn off the heat and add the cooked chicken and mixed veggies, along with the spicy red pepper sauce, Worcestershire sauce salt, and black pepper.
f) Add the shredded Gouda cheese and stir until everything is coated with sauce and spread evenly.
g) Liberally cover the dough with the mixture.
h) Grill the pizza or bake it for 18 minutes.

34) *Chicken Sausage and Apple Pizza*

Indulge in the perfect balance of savory and sweet with our Pizza featuring succulent Chicken Sausage and crisp Apples. Indulge in the delectable combination of savory chicken sausage, infused with aromatic herbs and spices, and crisp, thinly sliced apples atop a mouth-watering pizza crust. Experience the perfect balance of sweet and savory with our delicious apple and sausage pairing. The crisp texture of the apples perfectly complements the savory flavor of the sausage, creating a delightful crunch with every bite. Indulge in a mouth-watering medley of toppings, perfectly paired with a blend of cheeses - think velvety mozzarella or tangy goat cheese - for a truly decadent experience. Indulge in the perfect balance of savory and sweet with our Pizza featuring succulent Chicken Sausage and crisp Apples. This delectable dish showcases the true versatility of pizza as a canvas for a wide range of flavors.

Makes: 1 Large Pizza
Baking Time: 16 to 18 minutes

Ingredients:

- 1 tablespoon of extra virgin olive oil
- 1 green apple
- 6 ounces of shredded Fontina cheese
- 1½ ounces of grated Parmigiana, Pecorino, or Grana Padano cheese
- half pound of chicken or turkey sausage
- 2 teaspoons of finely chopped rosemary leaves

Instructions:

a) A 14-inch-diameter circle should be formed out of the dough by carefully turning and stretching it while holding the edges.
b) Warm up 1 tablespoon of olive oil in a skillet.
c) After thoroughly browning the chicken or turkey sausage, slice it into thin rounds.
d) Evenly cover the prepared crust with the ground mustard.
e) Spread the mustard with the shredded Fontina cheese.
f) Scatter the cut sausage evenly throughout the pizza.
g) Sprinkle fresh rosemary, cheese, and apple slices on top.
h) Grill the pizza for 16 to 18 minutes or bake it.

35) *Barbecue Chicken Pizza*

Experience the perfect blend of smoky and tangy flavors with our BBQ Chicken Pizza. Indulge in the deliciousness of barbecue on a pizza like never before. Indulge in our mouth-watering pizza variation that boasts of succulent chicken drenched in a delectable barbecue sauce, elevating the taste with a perfect blend of sweet and savory flavors. Indulge in the mouth-watering chicken dish, perfectly paired with a blend of premium cheeses like mozzarella or cheddar. The dish is then topped off with a delightful combination of red onions and cilantro, elevating the overall flavor profile to new heights. Indulge in the ultimate comfort food experience with our perfectly balanced pizza. Savor the delectable blend of tangy, smoky, and cheesy flavors that will leave you feeling completely satisfied. Indulge in the perfect fusion of two beloved cuisines with our BBQ Chicken Pizza. Savor the mouthwatering flavors of barbecue and pizza coming together in a delightful and crowd-pleasing combination.

Makes: 1 pizza
Baking Time: 16 to 18 minutes

Ingredients:
- One recipe for traditional Italian basic dough and flour for the pizza peel
- Six tablespoons of barbecue sauce
- 1 cup of cooked boneless chicken, sliced
- 4 ounces of shredded smoked provolone or smoked Swiss cheese
- 4 ounces of finely grated Parmigiana cheese
- 1 tea spoon of red pepper flakes (optional)
- ½ red onion, diced
- Chopped oregano leaves

Instructions:
a) A 14-inch-diameter circle should be formed out of the dough by carefully turning and stretching it while holding the edges.
b) Evenly smear the barbecue sauce over the prepared dough.
c) Top the sauce with the crumbled smoked cheese.
d) Arrange the sliced chicken pieces, diced red onion, and oregano leaves on top of the cheese.
e) If preferred, top with red pepper flakes.
f) Bake the pizza for 16 to 18 minutes or grill it.

CHAPTER 4: FISH AND SEAFOOD PIZZA

36) *Tuna Pizza*

Indulge in a tantalizing culinary experience with Tuna Pizza - a delectable twist on the classic pizza that tantalizes your taste buds with the fresh and invigorating flavors of the sea. Indulge in a mouth-watering pizza experience with our exquisite tuna variation. Savor the tender and flavorful tuna pieces, marinated in a blend of aromatic herbs and spices. The fresh ingredients of juicy tomatoes, crisp onions, and savory olives perfectly complement the tuna, creating a delectable symphony of flavors. Elevate your pizza experience with a touch of the Mediterranean! Our toppings are expertly finished with a delicate drizzle of premium olive oil and a sprinkle of fragrant herbs. Experience the delicate taste of tuna like never before with our light and flavorful pizza. Indulge in the delectable Tuna Pizza - a perfect pick for seafood aficionados and those looking for a healthier and lighter pizza alternative.

Makes: 1 Large Pizza
Baking Time: 15-20 minutes

Ingredients:
- One pre-baked pizza crust
- 8 ounces of melted cream cheese,
- 112 cups of shredded mozzarella cheese
- 5 ounces of drained and flaked tuna
- a half cup of sliced red onion
- Optional red pepper flakes

Instructions:
a) Spread the softened cream cheese over the cooked crust.
b) Top the cream cheese with the shredded mozzarella cheese.
c) Top with red onion slices, canned tuna, and red pepper flakes (if preferred).
d) Bake at 400 degrees Fahrenheit for 15 to 20 minutes.

37) *Mexican Shrimp Pizza*

Experience the bold and vibrant flavors of Mexican cuisine in every bite of our Pizza with Mexican Shrimp. Indulge in a mouth-watering pizza variation that boasts succulent shrimp seasoned with a tantalizing blend of Mexican spices, including cumin, chili powder, and paprika. Experience a burst of flavor with our succulent shrimp dish, served alongside a vibrant medley of bell peppers, onions, and jalapeños. The combination of these colorful ingredients creates a zesty and fiery kick that will tantalize your taste buds. Indulge in a mouthwatering medley of toppings, perfectly paired with a blend of delectable cheeses like Monterey Jack or queso fresco. A tantalizing twist of lime and a sprinkle of fresh cilantro completes this savory sensation. Indulge in a tantalizing pizza experience with our Mexican Shrimp Pizza. This delectable fusion of bold and fresh flavors will leave your taste buds craving for more.

Makes: 1 Large Pizza
Baking Time: 16 to 18 minutes

Ingredients:
- 1 traditional Italian recipe for a base Dough
- 1 jar of pickled jalapenos, seeded and chopped
- 6 ounces of shredded Cheddar cheese
- 6 ounces of steamed shrimp, peeled and deveined
- 1 shallot, chopped
- 8 ounces of cherry tomatoes, chopped
- 1 teaspoon of olive oil
- 1 teaspoon of red wine vinegar
- 1 teaspoon of cumin seeds
- 1½ table spoonful of chopped cilantro leaves
- A quarter teaspoon of salt

Instructions:
a) A 14-inch-diameter circle should be formed out of the dough by carefully turning and stretching it while holding the edges.
b) Combine chopped cilantro, shallot, salt, red wine vinegar, and cherry tomatoes in a bowl.
c) Apply this mixture to the crust that has been produced.
d) Top with crumbled Cheddar cheese.
e) Include the cooked, chopped shrimp along with the pickled jalapenos and cumin seeds.
f) For 16 to 18 minutes, grill or bake.

38) *Grilled shrimp pizzas*

Indulge in the delectable combination of smoky flavors and juicy seafood with our Grilled Shrimp Pizzas. Indulge in our mouth-watering pizza variation, featuring succulent grilled shrimp cooked to perfection. Savor the slightly charred and smoky taste that will leave your taste buds craving for more. Indulge in a delectable shrimp dish that's bursting with flavor! Our succulent shrimp is perfectly paired with an array of toppings, including savory roasted vegetables, crumbly feta cheese, and a tantalizing drizzle of tangy sauce or vinaigrette. Experience the perfect balance of textures with our crispy and golden crust, topped with a delicious array of toppings. Indulge in the ultimate culinary experience with our Grilled Shrimp Pizzas. Elevating the classic pizza to new heights, our gourmet twist features the mouthwatering versatility of succulent shrimp as a delectable topping.

Makes: 1 Serving
Baking Time: 10-15 minutes

Ingredients:
- 1 loaf of bread dough
- 1 cup of tomato sauce
- 1 pound of fresh shrimp.
- 6 ounces of shredded mozzarella cheese
- 1 cup of diced green bell pepper
- 12 cup sliced onion
- 2 chopped garlic cloves
- Two teaspoons of creole seasoning
- 1 teaspoon of vegetable oil
- 112 minced cloves of garlic
- A half cup of finely chopped Parmesan cheese

Instructions:
a) A 14-inch-diameter circle should be formed out of the dough by carefully turning and stretching it while holding the edges.
b) Before placing each ring of dough on the grill rack, brush 112 tea spoons of vegetable oil on one side of it.
c) Grill the rounds for 1-2 minutes per side.
d) Sauté the shrimp with the green bell pepper, sliced onion, minced garlic, and Creole spice in high oil.
e) Take out the shrimp from the pan, but continue to griddle the vegetable mixture.
f) Reintroduce the shrimp to the mixture after cutting them up.
g) Spread tomato sauce over the crusts that have been grilled, then add the shrimp and veggie combination on top.
h) Top with grated Parmesan and mozzarella cheese.
i) Grill for two minutes at 350°–400°F.

39) *White Clam Pizza*

Indulge in the savory flavors of Italy with our Pizza with White Clams. Inspired by the timeless dish of spaghetti alle vongole, this pizza masterpiece is a true culinary delight. Indulge in the succulent and savory flavors of our signature pizza variation. Delight in the tender and briny white clams, which are expertly steamed in a blend of white wine, garlic, and herbs. These delectable toppings are then artfully scattered atop a thin and crispy crust, creating a culinary masterpiece that is sure to tantalize your taste buds. Indulge in the delectable clams, served with a delicate and savory sauce, crafted with premium olive oil, garlic, and a dash of crushed red pepper flakes to add a tantalizing touch of spice. Experience the essence of the sea in every bite with our delicious pizza, where the natural sweetness of the clams shines through and leaves your taste buds craving for more. Indulge in the exquisite taste of the ocean with our Pizza with White Clams. This sophisticated flavor profile is sure to elevate your pizza experience and leave your taste buds craving more.

Makes: 1 Large Pizza
Baking Time: 14 - 16 Minutes

Ingredients:
- One recipe for an authentic Italian pizza crust
- Two table spoons of olive oil
- 12 ounces of cut clams
- half a tea spoon of red pepper flakes
- 6 minced garlic cloves
- Two teaspoons of dry white wine
- 112 ounces of coarsely grated Pecorino cheese;
- chopped parsley leaves

Instructions:
a) A 14-inch-diameter circle of dough should be rolled out and placed on a pizza peel or sheet pan by carefully turning and stretching the dough while holding the edges.
b) Get a skillet and heat the olive oil.
c) Sauté the minced garlic with the white wine, chopped clams, red pepper flakes, and parsley. For two minutes, simmer.
d) Top the prepared crust with the cooked contents.
e) Top with Pecorino cheese that has been coarsely grated.
f) For 14 to 16 minutes, grill or bake.

40) *Pissaladière, Pizza Style*

Indulge in the delectable Pizza-Style Pissaladière, a French delicacy with a tantalizing twist on the classic pizza. This savory dish hails from the charming region of Nice, and is sure to delight your taste buds. Indulge in our delectable pizza variation that boasts a thin and crispy crust, generously adorned with succulent caramelized onions, savory anchovies, and flavorful black olives. Indulge in the mouth-watering goodness of our pizza, where the onions are meticulously cooked to perfection, rendering a sweet and golden texture that imparts a rich and savory flavor to every bite. Experience the perfect balance of flavors with our anchovy and black olive combination. The briny and umami notes of the anchovies are perfectly complemented by the hint of bitterness and depth from the black olives. Indulge in the exquisite taste of Pizza-Style Pissaladière, a culinary masterpiece that brings together the best of French cuisine and pizza. Savor the sophisticated and elegant flavors that will tantalize your taste buds and leave you craving for more.

Makes: 1 Large Pizza
Baking Time: 14 - 16 Minutes

Ingredients:
- A single batch of the traditional Italian basic dough recipe.
- 3 ounces of tinned anchovy fillets,
- 1½ ounces of finely shredded Parmigiano cheese
- 2 table spoons of olive oil
- 18 pitted black olives
- A half pound of peeled Cipollini onions

Instructions:
a) A 14-inch-diameter circle should be formed out of the dough by carefully turning and stretching it while holding the edges.
b) Bake the peeled Cipollini onions for 50 minutes in the oven with the olive oil.
c) Dice the cooked onions, then distribute them throughout the dough.
d) Decorate the crust by arranging the anchovy fillets and black olives in a pleasing arrangement.
e) Cover everything with grated Parmigiano cheese.
f) For 14 to 16 minutes, grill or bake.

41) *Clams, Sausage, and Hazelnuts Pizza*

Experience a truly unforgettable pizza with our Clam, Sausage, and Hazelnut Pizza. The combination of these unexpected flavors will leave your taste buds craving more. Indulge in a mouthwatering pizza experience with our delectable variation. Our expertly crafted recipe combines tender clams, flavorful sausage, and crunchy hazelnuts for a perfect balance of textures and tastes. Indulge in the briny and oceanic flavors of the clams, perfectly complemented by the savory and meaty notes of the sausage. Experience the perfect balance of flavors and textures with our delicious hazelnuts. Their delightful crunch and subtle nuttiness perfectly complement the other ingredients, making every bite a truly satisfying experience. Indulge in the delectable taste of our Pizza with Clams, Sausage, and Hazelnuts - a true masterpiece that highlights the ingenuity and artistry of pizza toppings. Savor the distinct and luxurious flavor profile that this pizza has to offer.

Makes: 1 Large Pizza
Baking Time: 16-18 minutes

Ingredients:
- A single batch of the traditional Italian basic dough recipe.
- 6 tablespoons of chopped, toasted, peeled hazelnuts
- 6 ounces of shredded Manchego cheese
- A half teaspoon of sweet smoked paprika
- 10 ounces of chopped, tinned baby clams, drained, and rinsed;
- 4 ounces of dry Spanish chorizo;
- 1 onion, diced;

Instructions:
a) A 14-inch-diameter circle should be formed out of the dough by carefully turning and stretching it while holding the edges.
b) Sprinkle the crust with the shredded Manchego cheese.
c) Combine the diced red onion and smoked sweet paprika in a bowl, then top the crust with the combination.
d) Scatter the hazelnuts on top, chopped.
e) Distribute the dry Spanish chorizo in equal amounts.
f) Spread clams and hazelnuts evenly across the pizza.
g) For 16 to 18 minutes, bake or grill.

42) *Italian Smoked Salmon Pizza*

Indulge in the luxurious twist of our Italian Smoked Salmon Pizza, a delectable take on the classic pizza. Indulge in the exquisite flavors of our Italian smoked salmon pizza. Delicately sliced and smoky, our salmon is perfectly complemented by a creamy blend of mascarpone and cream cheese. Savor every bite of this delectable variation. Elevate your dish with a burst of freshness from a squeeze of tangy lemon juice and a sprinkle of savory capers and dill. These flavorful toppings will add a zesty and herbaceous touch that will tantalize your taste buds. Indulge in a pizza that exudes sophistication and taste. Our salmon pizza boasts a perfect balance of rich, buttery salmon and a crispy crust that will tantalize your taste buds. Indulge in a gourmet and sophisticated pizza experience with our Italian Smoked Salmon Pizza. This unique option offers a tantalizing twist on the classic pizza, perfect for those seeking a truly indulgent meal.

Makes: 1 Large Pizza
Baking Time: 14 - 16 Minutes

Ingredients:
- A single batch of the traditional Italian basic dough recipe.
- 2 tablespoons of room temperature cream cheese
- 4 sliced medium shallots
- 2 tea spoons of lemon juice - 12 tea spoon of freshly crushed black pepper
- ¼ cup of sour cream - 1 table spoon of fresh dill - 1 table spoon of olive oil
- Sliced, smoked salmon weighing 4 ounces
- 1 tablespoon of capers that have been rinsed and drained.

Instructions:
a) A 14-inch-diameter circle should be formed out of the dough by carefully turning and stretching it while holding the edges.
b) Top with the sliced shallots. The crust after evenly sprinkling olive oil over it.
c) Add freshly cracked black pepper to the dish.
d) Grill for 14 to 16 minutes or bake.
e) Combine the sour cream, cream cheese, capers that have been washed and drained, dill, and lemon juice in a bowl until the mixture is spreadable.
f) Distribute this mixture over the hot crust evenly.
g) Before slicing and serving, garnish with thinly sliced chunks of smoked salmon.

43) *White Bean with Tuna Pizza*

Indulge in the perfect blend of hearty legumes and delicate tuna flavors with our Pizza featuring White Beans and Tuna. This nutritious option is sure to satisfy your cravings while keeping you feeling full and energized. Indulge in a luxurious pizza experience with our latest variation! Our creamy white bean spread serves as the perfect base, delivering a smooth and velvety texture that will leave your taste buds craving for more. Indulge in the ultimate pizza experience with our delectable spread, generously topped with tender flakes of protein-packed tuna. Elevate your taste buds with the addition of sliced red onions, Kalamata olives, and fresh herbs. These toppings not only enhance the flavor profile but also provide a vibrant and refreshing touch to your dish. Indulge in the delectable Pizza with White Beans and Tuna, a wholesome and unique option that highlights the versatility of pizza as a conduit for nutritious ingredients without compromising on taste.

Makes: 1 Large Pizza
Baking Time: 16 to 18 minutes

Ingredients:
- A single batch of the traditional Italian basic dough recipe.
- 1¼ cups of rinsed and drained canned white beans
- 7 ounces of drained canned tuna
- 3 tablespoons of finely chopped parsley, sage, or oregano leaves
- 2 tablespoons of extra virgin olive oil
- 3 ounces of grana padano or Parmigiano cheese that has been shaved
- ½ medium lemon juice

Instructions:
a) A 14-inch-diameter circle should be formed out of the dough by carefully turning and stretching it while holding the edges.
b) Combine the tuna, chopped herbs, and canned white beans in a bowl.
c) Evenly distribute the ingredients over the dough.
d) Drizzle lemon juice and olive oil over the tuna and beans.
e) For 16 to 18 minutes, grill or bake.

44) *Puttanesca Pizza*

Indulge in the savory and daring flavors of Pizza Puttanesca - a tantalizing twist on the classic Italian dish. Experience the bold and robust taste of puttanesca sauce, now in the form of a mouth-watering pizza. Indulge in a mouthwatering pizza experience with our delectable variation. Our savory tomato sauce is infused with a tantalizing blend of anchovies, garlic, capers, and olives, making every bite a burst of flavor. Indulge in the rich and tangy sauce that serves as the perfect base for your pizza. Experience a burst of umami and briny flavors that will tantalize your taste buds. Indulge in a mouthwatering medley of toppings, perfectly paired with a delectable blend of cheeses, including the likes of mozzarella or Parmesan. To top it off, savor the added touch of fresh basil or oregano. Indulge in the ultimate pizza experience with our savory and satisfying creation. Our expertly crafted pizza boasts a medley of intense and complex flavors that will tantalize your taste buds. Indulge in the rich and robust flavors of our Pizza Puttanesca, a delectable choice for those who crave a pizza that's bursting with bold and distinctive taste sensations.

Makes: 1 Large Pizza
Baking Time: 16 to 18 minutes

Ingredients:
- 12 ounces of chopped Roma tomatoes;
- 12 tea spoon of red pepper flakes;
- 1 recipe for traditional Italian basic dough;
- 1 jar of chopped whole pimientos;
- 2 tins of chopped anchovy fillets;
- 4 ounces of grated Parmigiano cheese;
- 1 tea spoon of finely chopped oregano;
- ¼ tea spoon of salt;
- 2 minced garlic cloves;
- ¼ cup of chopped pitted black olives;
- ¼ cup of onion, diced;
- 1 tablespoon of chopped capers;
- ¼ tea spoon of rosemary leaves.

Instructions:
a) A 14-inch-diameter circle should be formed out of the dough by carefully turning and stretching it while holding the edges.
b) Sprinkle ¾ of the grated Parmigiano cheese over the prepared crust.
c) Combine the salt, red pepper flakes, Roma tomato chunks, pimiento chunks, anchovy fillet chunks, minced garlic, black olive chunks, diced onion, chopped capers, oregano, and rosemary leaves in a bowl.
d) Distribute this mixture over the cheese over the crust in an even layer.
e) For 16 to 18 minutes, grill or bake.

CHAPTER 5: VEGETABLE PIZZA

45) *Yellow Tomatoes White Pizza*

Experience a burst of flavor with our Pizza featuring Yellow Tomatoes. This vibrant twist on traditional tomato-based pizzas is sure to tantalize your taste buds. Indulge in a delectable pizza crust adorned with luscious slices of ripe yellow tomatoes, boasting a subtly sweet and gentle taste in contrast to their red counterparts. Experience a burst of sunshine on your pizza with our yellow tomatoes. These vibrant beauties add a pop of color and a subtle tanginess that will elevate your taste buds to new heights. Enhance your pizza experience with the perfect toppings - fresh basil leaves, creamy mozzarella cheese, and a tantalizing drizzle of olive oil. Experience a visually stunning and refreshingly delicious pizza that perfectly showcases the unique flavors of yellow tomatoes. Experience the freshness and vibrancy of our Yellow Tomato Pizza - a fantastic choice for pizza lovers!

Makes: 2 pizzas
Baking Time: about 12 minutes

Ingredients:
- Two traditional Italian dough recipes
- 2 sliced, ripe yellow tomatoes
- 8 basil leaves, fresh
- 1 Yukon Gold potato, sliced after being peeled
- Salt and freshly ground black pepper
- 1 sliced Vidalia onion
- 2 teaspoons of extra virgin olive oil

Instructions:
a) Season the potatoes with salt and pepper and bake for 10 minutes at 450 degrees Fahrenheit.
b) Gently move the dough to a pizza peel or oiled sheet pan.
c) In one tablespoon of olive oil, caramelize the onion. Add the oregano, salt, and pepper, and set aside.
d) Pour the remaining 1 tablespoon of olive oil over the pizza dough that has been prepared.
e) Cover the dough with the caramelized onion.
f) Garnish with basil leaves, tomato and potato slices, and potatoes.
g) 12 minutes in the oven.

46) *Cheese Sauce Broccoli Pizza*

Indulge in the ultimate comfort food with our Cheese-Sauce Pizza with Broccoli. This mouth-watering delight combines the creamy richness of a delectable cheese sauce with the wholesome goodness of fresh broccoli. Satisfy your cravings with every cheesy bite. Indulge in a mouthwatering pizza experience with our signature recipe. A delectable pizza crust is generously smothered with a velvety cheese sauce, crafted from a blend of premium melted cheeses such as cheddar, mozzarella, or Gruyere. Indulge in the luxurious base of our pizza, where the sauce provides a velvety texture and a burst of cheesy flavor. Indulge in the ultimate pizza experience with our mouth-watering creation, topped with delicate broccoli florets that provide a delightful crunch and a subtle hint of earthy goodness. Elevate your taste buds with our selection of premium toppings including diced onions, garlic, and herbs. Indulge in the ultimate comfort food with our creamy broccoli pizza, bursting with the perfect blend of cheese and broccoli. Indulge in the delectable Cheese-Sauce Pizza with Broccoli, a perfect pick for those seeking a scrumptious and savory vegetarian delight.

Makes: 1 Large Pizza
Baking Time: 10-15 minutes

Ingredients:

- One traditional Italian basic dough recipe
- 2 teaspoons of flour
- Six ounces of finely grated Cheddar cheese
- 2 ounces of Parmigiano or Grana Padano cheese, finely grated
- One teaspoon of Dijon mustard
- 1¼ cups milk
- 1 tea spoon of thyme leaves with stems
- 2 teaspoons of butter
- One-half teaspoon of salt
- 3 sprinklings of hot red pepper sauce
- 3 cups of broccoli florets, steamed

Instructions:

a) Holding the edges, carefully rotate and stretch the dough into a circle with a 14-inch diameter.
b) In a saucepan, melt the butter and whisk in the flour until the substance turns light blonde. Whisk in the milk gradually.
c) After removing the pan from the heat, combine the shredded Cheddar cheese, spicy red pepper sauce, Dijon mustard, stemmed thyme leaves, salt, and cheese until well combined.
d) Grill the crust for 15 minutes or bake it.
e) Let the gooey cheese sauce cool completely before slathering it on top of the crust.
f) Sprinkle steamed broccoli florets on top of the pizza.

47) *Tomato Sauce with Broccoli Pizza*

Indulge in the timeless and mouth-watering pairing of Tomato Sauce with Broccoli Pizza. The tangy tomato sauce perfectly complements the vibrant broccoli, making every bite a burst of flavor. Indulge in a mouthwatering pizza experience with our signature recipe. Our crispy pizza crust is generously topped with a delectable tomato sauce, infused with a blend of fresh tomatoes, garlic, herbs, and spices. Indulge in the mouth-watering pizza with a rich and robust tomato sauce that adds depth of flavor and a perfect touch of acidity. Experience the perfect pizza indulgence with our deliciously crafted pizza, topped with your choice of fresh or roasted broccoli florets. The slight crunch and delightful earthy taste of the broccoli will leave your taste buds craving for more. Elevate your taste experience by adding delectable toppings like cheese, olives, or red onions to your dish. Indulge in a pizza that not only satisfies your cravings but also nourishes your body. The natural sweetness of the tomatoes perfectly complements the vibrant broccoli, resulting in a truly satisfying experience. Indulge in the timeless and nourishing Tomato Sauce with Broccoli Pizza - a perfect pick for pizza lovers!

Makes: 1 Large Pizza
Baking Time: 16 to 18 minutes

Ingredients:
- 3 ounces of grated Havarti or Provolone cheese
- One traditional Italian basic dough recipe
- 1 roasted red pepper or pimento in a jar
- A tea spoon's worth of red pepper flakes
- A cup and a half of pizza sauce
- Three ounces of finely grated mozzarella cheese
- 1 ounce of Grana Padano or Parmigiano cheese that has been finely grated
- 2 cups of florets of steaming broccoli

Instructions:
a) Holding the edges, carefully rotate and stretch the dough into a circle with a 14-inch diameter.
b) Pulverize the pimiento or roasted red pepper.
c) Evenly cover the prepared crust with the pizza sauce.
d) Top with some provolone or havarti cheese that has been shred.
e) Include some red pepper flakes and shredded mozzarella cheese.
f) Place the florets of steamed broccoli on top of the crust.
g) Dot the pizza with the pimiento puree.
h) Top with the finely shredded Grana Padano or Parmigiano cheese.
i) For 16 to 18 minutes, grill or bake.

48) *Chard Pizza*

Indulge in a one-of-a-kind pizza experience with Chard Pizza. Our pizzas are not only delicious, but also packed with nutrition thanks to the incorporation of fresh chard leaves. Indulge in a mouthwatering pizza crust, generously topped with sautéed chard perfectly seasoned with garlic, premium olive oil, and a dash of salt and pepper. Experience the delightful bitterness and vibrant green hue of chard leaves on your pizza. Elevate your taste experience with our delectable toppings including savory cheese, perfectly caramelized onions, and succulent roasted red peppers. Experience a visually stunning pizza that bursts with the rich, earthy flavors of chard. Indulge in the deliciousness of pizza while incorporating more leafy greens into your diet with the fantastic choice of Chard Pizza.

Makes: 1
Baking Time: 16 to 18 minutes

Ingredients:
- 4 cups of Swiss chard leaves, stemmed and shred
- One traditional Italian basic dough recipe
- Unsalted butter, two tablespoons
- A tea spoonful of freshly grated nutmeg
- 3 minced garlic cloves
- Six ounces of finely grated mozzarella cheese
- ⅓ cup of shredded Roquefort or Gorgonzola cheese
- A tea spoon's worth of red pepper flakes

Instructions:
a) Holding the edges, carefully rotate and stretch the dough into a circle with a 14-inch diameter.
b) Melt the butter in a skillet and sauté the minced garlic for one minute.
c) Stirring often, sauté the Swiss chard leaves in the skillet for 4 minutes after shredding and removing the stems.
d) Cover the dough with the shredded Mozzarella cheese.
e) Sprinkle crumbled Gorgonzola or Roquefort cheese and the cooked Swiss chard mixture on top of the pizza.
f) Grate some nutmeg and top with red pepper flakes.
g) For 16 to 18 minutes, grill or bake.

49) *Peas and Carrots Pizza*

Indulge in a playful and colorful pizza variation with our Peas and Carrots Pizza. This delectable dish brings together the sweet flavors of peas and tender carrots for a truly unique taste experience. Indulge in a mouthwatering pizza experience with our delectable recipe. Our signature pizza crust is generously layered with a rich tomato sauce and topped with a delightful combination of tender peas and carrots. These veggies are cooked to perfection, bringing out their natural sweetness and adding a burst of flavor to every bite. Elevate your pizza experience with a variety of delectable toppings such as creamy cheese, fragrant herbs, or a tantalizing drizzle of olive oil. Experience a visually stunning pizza bursting with the fresh flavors of the garden. Indulge in a one-of-a-kind and nourishing pizza adventure with our Peas and Carrots Pizza. This delightful pie pays homage to the lively and delectable taste of veggies, making it a fantastic choice for any foodie looking for something extraordinary.

Makes: 1
Baking Time: 10-15 minutes

Ingredients:

- One traditional Italian basic dough recipe
- 1 and a half tablespoons of flour
- A quarter cup of coconut milk
- Three ounces of thick cream
- Unsalted butter, two tablespoons
- 2 tea spoons of thyme leaves with stems
- A tea spoonful of freshly grated nutmeg
- 1 cup of peas in shells
- 1 cup of carrots, diced
- 3 minced garlic cloves
- 1 ounce of your preferred type of finely grated cheese

Instructions:

a) Holding the edges, carefully rotate and stretch the dough into a circle with a 14-inch diameter.
b) Melt the butter in a skillet, then whisk in the flour until the mixture is smooth and a very light beige color.
c) While whisking, slowly and gradually stream in the coconut milk.
d) Combine the heavy cream, cheese that has been grated, nutmeg, and stemmed thyme leaves.
e) Grill the crust for ten minutes or bake it.
f) Cover the crust with the coconut milk-based sauce.
g) Sprinkle the sauce with the chopped garlic, peas, and carrots.
h) Sprinkle the cheese that has been finely grated over the tops.

50) *Potato, Chutney with Monterey Jack Pizza*

Experience a mouthwatering fusion of Indian and American flavors with our Potato Chutney with Monterey Jack Pizza. Savor the creamy and tangy goodness of potato chutney perfectly paired with the meltingly delicious Monterey Jack cheese. Indulge in a delectable pizza crust that's generously layered with a tantalizing blend of spiced potato chutney. This savory chutney is crafted using a medley of boiled and mashed potatoes, aromatic spices, and fragrant herbs. Indulge in the rich and velvety chutney that serves as the perfect foundation for your pizza. Indulge in the mouthwatering goodness of our dish, crowned with luscious Monterey Jack cheese that melts to perfection, elevating the flavors to a whole new level of richness and savoriness. Enhance the texture and flavor of your dish by adding some delightful toppings like diced onions, bell peppers, or cilantro. Indulge in a pizza that boasts a luscious, rich texture and a burst of delectable flavors. Experience the perfect fusion of Indian and American culinary artistry in every bite. Indulge in a truly unique and adventurous pizza experience with our Potato Chutney with Monterey Jack Pizza. This delectable choice combines the best of both worlds, delivering a flavor explosion that will leave your taste buds begging for more.

Makes: 1
Baking Time: 16 to 18 minutes

Ingredients:
- One traditional Italian basic dough recipe
- 3-tablespoon servings of finely chopped dill fronds
- 6 teaspoons of fruit chutney
- Grated Monterey Jack cheese, 6 ounces
- 12 ounces of sliced, steam-cooked white potatoes
- 1 sliced Vidalia onion

Instructions:
a) Holding the edges, carefully rotate and stretch the dough into a circle with a 14-inch diameter.
b) Cover the prepared crust with the fruit chutney in an even layer.
c) Evenly strew the top with shredded Monterey Jack cheese.
d) Add chopped dill fronds on top of the layered potatoes and pizza.
e) Slice the onions into strips and place them in a pattern on top of the pizza.
f) For 16 to 18 minutes, bake or grill.

51) *Roasted Roots Pizza*

Indulge in the savory and satisfying Roasted Roots Pizza, a delectable variation that pays homage to the rich and earthy flavors of roasted root vegetables. Indulge in a mouth-watering pizza crust adorned with a medley of roasted root vegetables, including delectable carrots, beets, parsnips, and sweet potatoes. Indulge in a mouthwatering medley of vegetables, drizzled with premium olive oil and seasoned with a blend of aromatic herbs and spices. Roasted to perfection, each bite is a delectable balance of tender texture and rich, caramelized flavor. Indulge in a delightful blend of flavors and textures as the natural sweetness of the roasted roots perfectly complements the crispy crust and melted cheese. The result is a medley that will tantalize your taste buds. Elevate your taste buds with our selection of premium toppings including tangy goat cheese, fragrant fresh herbs, and a delectable drizzle of balsamic glaze. Indulge in the delicious and wholesome Roasted Roots Pizza, perfect for those seeking a veggie-packed slice without compromising on taste. Savor the rich and delightful flavors in every bite, while feeling good about your healthy choice.

Makes: 1
Baking Time: about 16 minutes

Ingredients:
- One traditional Italian basic dough recipe
- 1 teaspoon balsamic vinegar
- 4 ounces of mozzarella cheese, shredded
- 1 ounce of freshly grated Parmigiano-Reggiano
- One-half teaspoon of salt
- A half head of garlic
- ½ sliced and peeled parsnip
- ½ sliced and peeled sweet potato
- ½ a sliced and half fennel bulb
- One tablespoon of olive oil

Instructions:
a) Holding the edges, carefully rotate and stretch the dough into a circle with a 14-inch diameter.
b) Wrap the unpeeled garlic cloves in foil and grill them over high heat for 40 minutes.
c) Combine the sweet potatoes, parsnips, and fennel with salt and oil.
d) Spread the vegetables out across a large sheet pan and roast for 15 to 20 minutes, or until tender.
e) Sprinkle shredded mozzarella over the prepared crust.
f) Top the cheese with the roasted vegetables.
g) Spread the mushy, pulpy garlic cloves on the pizza.
h) Top with the grated Parmigiano.
i) Carefully move the dough from the peel to the grill or oven for pizza.
j) 16 minutes on the grill or in the oven.

52) *Arugula salad pizza*

Experience the perfect blend of crispy pizza crust and vibrant arugula salad with our Arugula Salad Pizza. Savor the bright and fresh flavors of this delicious pizza variation. Indulge in the ultimate pizza experience with our mouth-watering recipe. Our signature pizza crust is perfectly complemented by a layer of tangy tomato sauce, topped off with a generous handful of fresh arugula leaves. Savor every bite of this delectable creation! Experience the perfect balance of flavors with our delicious pizza topped with fresh arugula. The peppery and slightly bitter taste of the arugula perfectly complements the rich and savory flavors of the pizza. Elevate your pizza experience with delectable toppings like shaved Parmesan cheese, juicy cherry tomatoes, or a tantalizing drizzle of balsamic glaze. Indulge in a pizza that is not only light and refreshing but also bursting with flavor. Indulge in the delectable Arugula Salad Pizza, a perfect pick for those who crave a veggie-packed and lighter pizza alternative. This pizza is a harmonious blend of textures and flavors that will tantalize your taste buds.

Makes: 1
Baking Time: 30-35 minutes

Ingredients:
- One whole-wheat pizza crust
- 1 teaspoon balsamic vinegar
- One-third cup of marinara sauce
- 2 cups of baby spinach and fresh arugula
- 1 sliced avocado
- 1 ½ cups of cherry tomatoes, halved
- 1 cup of vegan cheese that has been diced
- ½ chopped red bell pepper
- 1½ tea spoons of dried oregano
- roasted pistachios, ¼ cup

Instructions:
a) Set the pizza oven's temperature to 350 °F.
b) Roll out the pizza dough and set it on top of a pan or stone that has been dusted with cornmeal.
c) Spoon the Marinara sauce, oregano, and vegan cheese over the dough.
d) The crust should be baked for 30 to 35 minutes.
e) Arrange arugula, baby spinach, tomatoes, bell peppers, avocado, and toasted pistachios on top of the pizza as a garnish.
f) Drizzle balsamic vinegar and olive oil over the pizza.

53) *Caramelized Onion Pizza*

Indulge in the savory and rich flavors of our Caramelized Onion Pizza. This delectable choice showcases the sweetness of caramelized onions, making it a truly indulgent experience. Indulge in a mouth-watering pizza crust that's adorned with a lavish serving of caramelized onions. These onions are cooked to perfection, low and slow, until they transform into a rich, golden brown hue that's bursting with flavor. Experience the natural sweetness and delightful aroma of our pizza, enhanced by the addition of fresh onions. Elevate your dish with a variety of delectable toppings like tangy goat cheese, fragrant thyme, or a tantalizing drizzle of balsamic glaze that perfectly complement the rich flavors of caramelized onions. Indulge in a pizza that boasts a perfect balance of sweet and savory flavors, leaving you feeling completely satisfied. The onions steal the show, adding a deliciously bold and irresistible taste. Indulge in the ultimate comfort food with our Caramelized Onion Pizza. Bursting with flavor, this pizza is sure to satisfy your cravings and leave you feeling satisfied.

Makes: 1
Baking Time: 10-15 minutes

Ingredients:
- One traditional Italian basic dough recipe
- Two tablespoons of oil for drizzling
- 6 cloves of garlic
- 3-tablespoon servings of fresh thyme
- 1 tablespoon of draining capers
- 6-cups worth of thinly chopped onions
- For frying onions, use ¼ cup of olive oil
- A bay leaf
- Pepper and salt
- Pine nuts, 1½ table spoons

Instructions:
a) Add the onions, garlic, thyme, and bay leaf to a pan that has been heated with 1/4 cup of olive oil.
b) Cook for 45 minutes, or until all the moisture is gone.
c) Discard the bay leaf and add salt and pepper to taste.
d) Cover the dough with the caramelized onion mixture.
e) Top with the remaining olive oil, capers, and pine nuts for decoration.
f) Ten minutes in the oven.

54) *Griddle spinach pizza*

Indulge in the delectable Griddled Spinach Pizza, a one-of-a-kind pizza variation that highlights the lively and bold flavors of sautéed spinach. Indulge in a mouthwatering pizza crust that's cooked to perfection on a stovetop, resulting in a crispy and slightly charred texture. Indulge in the delectable griddled crust, perfectly complemented by a layer of sautéed spinach, garlic, and olive oil. Experience the freshness of spinach and the delightful crunch of griddled crust with our delicious pizza. Elevate your taste experience by adding delectable toppings like creamy mozzarella cheese, zesty red pepper flakes, or juicy sliced tomatoes. Indulge in a mouthwatering pizza that not only satiates your cravings but also nourishes your body. The spinach topping adds a pop of vibrant green goodness that will leave your taste buds wanting more. Indulge in the delectable Griddled Spinach Pizza, a perfect pick for those seeking an unparalleled and savory pizza adventure that pays homage to the purity of natural ingredients.

Makes: 1
Baking Time: 8 minutes

Ingredients:
- One-fourth cup of marinara sauce
- ¼ cup of spinach, finely chopped
- 1 cup of desired cheese crumbles
- ¼ cup of halved cherry tomatoes
- One-eighth teaspoon of oregano

Instructions:
a) In a bowl, add the flour, water, oil, and salt; whisk to blend.
b) Coat a heated griddle with cooking spray before adding the batter to it.
c) Cook each side for 4 minutes.
d) Turn the crust over once more, then sprinkle oregano, cheese crumbles, spinach, cherry tomatoes, and marinara sauce over top.

55) *Garden Fresh Pizza*

Indulge in the delightful and wholesome Garden Fresh Pizza, a delectable variation that showcases the abundance of fresh vegetables straight from the garden. Indulge in a mouth-watering pizza crust that is adorned with a vibrant array of garden-fresh vegetables. From juicy bell peppers to succulent zucchini, plump tomatoes to earthy mushrooms, this recipe is a feast for the senses. Customize your pizza toppings to your liking - sautéed, grilled, or raw. It's all about your personal taste. Elevate your pizza experience with the addition of fresh herbs, premium cheese, or a tantalizing drizzle of olive oil. Experience a pizza like no other, bursting with vibrant flavors, textures, and colors that will tantalize your taste buds. Indulge in the ultimate pizza experience with Garden Fresh Pizza - a delectable choice that celebrates the abundant harvest of the garden while providing a wholesome and savory treat for your taste buds.

Makes: 2
Baking Time: about 10 minutes

Ingredients:
- Two 8-ounce chilled crescent roll packages
- Cream cheese that has been softened, 16 ounces
- ⅓ cup mayonnaise
- 1¼ ounces of dried soup base for vegetables
- Raspberry slices
- 1 cup of chopped bell peppers in various colors
- 1 cup of broccoli and 1 cup of cauliflower
- ½ cup of chopped celery and carrots, respectively

Instructions:
a) Cover the bottom of a jellyroll pan with an even layer of crescent roll dough.
b) Use your fingers to pinch any seams together to form a crust.
c) Bake at 400°F for about 10 minutes.
d) Combine the mayonnaise, cream cheese, and vegetable soup mix.
e) Cover the crust with the cream cheese mixture.
f) Sprinkle sliced raspberries, minced bell peppers, broccoli, cauliflower, celery, and carrots on top of the pizza.
g) Overnight in the refrigerator.

56) *Roma Fontina Pizza*

Indulge in the mouth-watering Roma Fontina Pizza, a tantalizing pizza variation that perfectly captures the essence of Rome, Italy Indulge in a mouth-watering pizza experience with our signature recipe. Our crispy pizza crust is generously topped with juicy Roma tomatoes, premium Fontina cheese, and a tantalizing blend of authentic Italian herbs and spices. Savor every bite of this Italian-inspired masterpiece. Indulge in the delectable combination of Roma tomatoes' rich and sweet taste, perfectly complemented by the creamy and slightly nutty flavor of Fontina cheese. Indulge in the perfect balance of flavors with this harmonious combination of ingredients that will leave you feeling completely satisfied. Elevate your taste experience by adding fresh basil leaves, garlic, or prosciutto as delectable toppings. Indulge in the delectable flavors of Italy with our Roma Fontina Pizza. It's the perfect choice for those who crave an authentic Italian experience with every bite.

Makes: 2
Baking Time: 10-15 minutes

Ingredients:
- Two pre-baked 12-inch pizza crusts
- One-half teaspoon of sea salt
- ¼ cup olive oil
- 1 teaspoon of garlic, minced
- 8 oz. of grated mozzarella cheese
- ½ cup of chopped Feta cheese
- Grated Fontina cheese, 4 ounces
- ½ cup freshly grated Parmesan cheese
- 8 sliced Roma tomatoes
- Ten freshly torn basil leaves

Instructions:
a) Combine the sliced tomatoes, sea salt, olive oil, and crushed garlic in a bowl. Each pizza crust should have an even layer of this mixture on top.
b) Top the tomato mixture with a layer of Mozzarella and Fontina cheese. Then include the chopped tomatoes, minced basil, Parmesan, and crumbled feta cheese.
c) Cook the pizzas on the grill or in the oven for about 15 minutes at 400 degrees Fahrenheit.

57) *Spinach Artichoke Pizza*

Indulge in the delectable combination of creamy spinach and tangy artichoke flavors with our Spinach Artichoke Pizza. Indulge in a mouthwatering pizza experience with our signature recipe. Our pizza crust is generously topped with a luscious blend of spinach, artichoke hearts, cream cheese, and grated Parmesan, creating a creamy base that will tantalize your taste buds. Indulge in the luxurious and delectable creamy spinach and artichoke blend, generously spread over our perfectly crafted crust, creating a mouthwatering and savory foundation. Indulge in our mouth-watering pizza, crowned with a generous layer of mozzarella cheese that oozes and stretches with every bite. Indulge in a mouthwatering pizza that boasts a delectable blend of savory flavors and wholesome vegetables. Indulge in a truly unique pizza experience with our mouth-watering Spinach Artichoke Pizza. It's the perfect choice for those seeking a deliciously indulgent meal.

Makes: 2
Baking Time: about 8 minutes

Ingredients:
- 2 prepared pizza crusts
- ¼ cup of water
- 2 teaspoons nutritional yeast
- ½ cup cashews
- A pinch each of salt, pepper, and red pepper flakes
- One-half cup of mozzarella cheese
- One tablespoon of freshly squeezed lemon juice
- 1 can of washed and drained white beans
- 1 chopped onion
- Fresh spinach, 5 cups
- 2 minced garlic cloves
- 1 can of drained artichoke hearts

Instructions
a) Set the pizza oven's temperature to 350 °F.
b) Blend the white beans, cashews, water, nutritional yeast, and lemon juice until smooth.
c) Saute the finely chopped onion in heated oil in a skillet until transparent.
d) Cook for an additional three minutes after adding the chopped garlic and fresh spinach to the pan.
e) Add the white bean and cashew mixture after stirring. Add salt, black pepper, and red pepper flakes for seasoning.
f) Cover the pizza dough with the ingredients.
g) Quarter the artichoke hearts and scatter them across the pie.
h) Top with mozzarella cheese.
i) 8 minutes in the oven for the pizza.

58) *BBQ Pizza with Crispy Cauliflower*

Indulge in a delectable twist on classic barbecue flavors with our BBQ Pizza topped with Crispy Cauliflower. The crispy cauliflower crust serves as the perfect foundation for a mouthwatering medley of toppings. Experience the perfect blend of smoky and tangy flavors with our mouth-watering recipe that combines the goodness of barbecue sauce with the crispy texture of roasted cauliflower. Indulge in a guilt-free pizza experience with our golden and crispy roasted cauliflower crust, coated in tangy barbecue sauce. It's a nutritious and mouth-watering alternative to the traditional pizza crusts. Indulge in our mouth-watering pizza, generously topped with delectable barbecue sauce, gooey cheese, and a variety of toppings to choose from, including savory red onions, crisp bell peppers, or succulent cooked chicken. Indulge in a pizza that not only satiates your cravings but also tantalizes your taste buds with its distinctive flavors. Indulge in the mouth-watering BBQ Pizza with Crispy Cauliflower - a perfect pick for those who crave a gluten-free or veggie-packed pizza that doesn't compromise on flavor.

Makes: 2
Baking Time: 12-15 minutes

Ingredients:
- One traditional Italian basic dough recipe
FOR THE BARBECUE CAULIFLOWER:
- One teaspoon of powdered smoked paprika
- Cauliflower, ½ head, cut into florets
- One-half teaspoon of liquid smoke
- One cup of barbecue sauce

- One teaspoon of garlic powder
CONCERNING THE GARLIC SAUCE:
- 1 cup of coconut yogurt, plain
- 2 minced garlic cloves
- Black and white pepper

Instructions
a) Combine the BBQ sauce and smoked paprika powder in a bowl.
b) Coat the cauliflower florets by dipping them into half of the sauce.
c) Spread the coated florets out on a sheet pan and bake them at 350°F for 10 minutes.
d) Spread the pizza dough out and top it with the BBQ cauliflower and any extra BBQ sauce.
e) The pizza should be baked for 12 to 15 minutes.
f) Top with parsley and green onions.
g) Combine the ingredients for the garlic sauce in another bowl and drizzle.

59) *Grilled Veggie Pizza*

Indulge in the mouth-watering and nutritious Grilled Veggie Pizza, which perfectly captures the rich and smoky essence of grilled vegetables. Indulge in a mouth-watering pizza crust that's adorned with a vibrant array of grilled veggies including zucchini, bell peppers, eggplant, and onions. Indulge in the exquisite taste of our grilled vegetables, delicately brushed with premium olive oil and seasoned with a blend of aromatic herbs and spices. Savor the perfect balance of flavors and textures, as each bite takes you on a journey of culinary delight. Experience the rich and intricate flavors of our pizza, enhanced by the smoky and charred essence of our grilled vegetables. Elevate your pizza experience with the addition of premium ingredients such as tangy goat cheese, fragrant fresh herbs, or a tantalizing drizzle of balsamic glaze. Experience a pizza like no other - one that is bursting with flavor and packed with nutrients. Our secret? Grilled vegetables that steal the show and leave your taste buds wanting more. Indulge in the taste of summer with our Grilled Veggie Pizza. This vegetable-packed pizza is the perfect choice for those seeking a lighter, yet flavorful pizza experience.

Makes: 2 pizzas
Baking Time: 15 Minutes

Ingredients:
- 2 Pizza Crust Without Yeast
- **A TOPPING**
- 1 sliced red onion
- 5 cups of thinly sliced mushrooms
- One dash of salt
- ¾ cup of cheese crumbles
- One teaspoon of olive oil
- ½ sliced zucchini
- 1 chopped red bell pepper

Instructions
a) Adjust the temperature of the pizza oven to 480°F.
b) Sauté the diced red onion, red bell pepper, mushrooms, and zucchini in olive oil in a pan.
c) Salt the vegetables lightly and boil them until they are tender.
d) Split the pizza dough in half, then lay out each portion on a sheet of parchment paper that has been lightly dusted with flour.
e) Cover the dough with tomato sauce. Sprinkle cheese slivers and the cooked vegetables on top.
f) Olive oil the crust by brushing it with it.
g) The pizzas should bake for around 15 minutes.

60) *Artichoke & Olive Pizza*

Indulge in the savory and exotic Artichoke & Olive Pizza, a Mediterranean-inspired masterpiece that tantalizes your taste buds with the perfect blend of briny artichokes and olives atop a delectable pizza crust. Indulge in the savory flavors of our pizza masterpiece. Our crispy crust is smothered with a rich tomato sauce, then adorned with tender artichoke hearts and a medley of olives, including the exquisite Kalamata and the succulent green olive. Experience the delicate and slightly tangy taste of artichokes, perfectly complemented by a burst of briny flavor from the olives. Indulge in a one-of-a-kind pizza experience with our carefully crafted combination of premium ingredients. Elevate your taste experience with our selection of premium toppings, including tangy feta cheese, savory red onions, and fragrant fresh basil. Indulge in the savory and exotic taste of our Artichoke & Olive Pizza, a perfect pick for pizza enthusiasts who crave a Mediterranean-inspired twist on classic pizza flavors.

Makes: 1
Baking Time: 8-10 minutes

Ingredients:
- A 12-inch prebaked pizza crust
- 1 cup of cheese crumbles
- 2 ounces of drained and diced black olives
- One-half cup of pesto
- Chopped red onion, half
- 1 chopped tomato
- A half cup of finely chopped green bell pepper
- 4 ounces of sliced, drained artichoke hearts

Instructions:
a) Set the pizza crust on a substantial pan.
b) Spread pesto over the crust, then sprinkle the cheese and vegetables in chunks on top of that.
c) Top the pizza with extra cheese.
d) Bake the pizza at 450 degrees Fahrenheit for 8 to 10 minutes.

61) *Potato and burrata pizza*

Indulge in the luxurious flavors of our Potato and Burrata Pizza. This delectable variation showcases the creamy and delicate notes of burrata cheese and perfectly roasted potatoes. Indulge in a mouthwatering pizza crust adorned with delicate slices of roasted potatoes, generously sprinkled with creamy burrata cheese and finished with a touch of fragrant herbs. Experience the perfect combination of tender and slightly caramelized potatoes on your pizza, adding a delightful texture and sweetness to every bite. Indulge in the luxurious creaminess of burrata cheese as it delicately envelops the tender potatoes, resulting in a decadent and opulent flavor experience. Elevate your pizza experience with the addition of flavorful ingredients such as aromatic garlic, fragrant rosemary, or a tantalizing drizzle of premium olive oil. Indulge in the ultimate comfort food with our decadent pizza. The perfect combination of creamy burrata cheese and savory potatoes will leave your taste buds craving more.

Makes: 4
Baking Time: 10-15 minutes

Ingredients:
- ½ pound No-Knead Pizza Dough and Bread Dough
- One-third cup of Lemon Basil Pesto
- ⅓ cup of white cheddar cheese, shredded
- Leaves of basil and thyme, for garnish
- 1 sliced thin potato
- Olive oil extra-virgin
- Two tablespoons of Everything Bagel Spice
- 8 ounces of shredded burrata cheese

Instructions:
a) Lower the temperature of the pizza oven to 450°F.
b) On a surface that has been lightly dusted with flour, roll out the dough.
c) Carefully move the dough to a greased baking sheet.
d) Spread pesto evenly over the dough.
e) Add cheddar cheese and potato slices on top.
f) Sprinkle everything bagel seasoning and drizzle with olive oil.
g) Bake the goods for 10–15 minutes.
h) Sprinkle fresh basil, thyme leaves, and torn burrata cheese on top of the pizza.

62) *Chard and Squash Pizza*

Indulge in the vibrant and flavorful Chard and Squash Pizza, a delectable variation that pays homage to the bounty of seasonal vegetables. Indulge in a mouthwatering pizza experience with our latest recipe. Our signature pizza crust is adorned with a delectable combination of sautéed Swiss chard and roasted butternut squash. A generous sprinkling of cheese adds the perfect finishing touch to this culinary masterpiece. Experience a delightful blend of flavors with our Swiss chard and roasted butternut squash dish. The Swiss chard offers a subtle bitterness and earthy notes, perfectly complemented by the natural sweetness and creamy texture of the roasted butternut squash. Indulge in a symphony of flavors and textures with the perfect combination of these wholesome ingredients. Satisfy your cravings while nourishing your body with every bite. Enhance the flavor of your dish by adding delectable toppings like caramelized onions, crumbly feta cheese, or crunchy toasted pine nuts. Indulge in the ultimate vegetable-forward and seasonally-inspired pizza experience with our Chard and Squash Pizza. It's a fantastic choice that will leave your taste buds craving for more.

Makes: 1 Large Pizza
Baking Time: 16 to 18 minutes

Ingredients:
- One traditional Italian basic dough recipe
- A quarter cup of dry white wine
- One tablespoon of maple syrup
- 1 chopped yellow onion
- One cup of delicata squash dice
- 4 cups of Swiss chard leaves, chopped
- One-half teaspoon of freshly cracked black pepper
- One teaspoon of finely chopped sage leaves
- ½ tea spoon cinnamon, ground
- one tablespoon of unsalted butter
- Salt, ½ tea spoon
- 8 ounces of finely chopped Fontina cheese

Instructions:
a) Gently rotate and stretch the dough into a 14-inch-diameter circle.
b) In a skillet, heat the butter before adding the diced squash and chopped onion. seven minutes to cook.
c) Add the chard after pouring the white wine.
d) Continue to stir until the sage, black pepper, cinnamon, and maple syrup are added, and stir until the sage is only partially wilted.
e) Simmer for approximately 8 minutes.
f) Scatter the shredded Fontina cheese evenly on the crust.
g) Top the cheese with the squash and chard topping.
h) For 16 to 18 minutes, bake or grill.

63) *Avocado, Olives & Mushroom Pizza*

Indulge in the mouth-watering Avocado, Olives & Mushroom Pizza - a delectable blend of rich and creamy avocado, savory olives, and hearty mushrooms. This unique combination is sure to tantalize your taste buds and leave you craving for more. Indulge in a mouth-watering pizza experience with our latest recipe. Our signature pizza crust is generously topped with creamy mashed avocado, savory sliced black olives, and perfectly sautéed mushrooms. A sprinkle of cheese adds the perfect finishing touch to this delectable dish. Indulge in the rich and velvety texture of mashed avocado, perfectly complemented by the bold and zesty flavor of olives. Indulge in the savory and robust flavor of sautéed mushrooms that add a meaty texture to your pizza. Experience the ultimate pizza indulgence with our carefully crafted combination of ingredients that deliver a burst of umami flavors in every bite. Elevate your pizza experience with our selection of premium toppings, including fresh herbs, zesty red pepper flakes, and a tangy squeeze of lemon juice. Enhance the overall taste and take your taste buds on a journey with every bite. Indulge in a one-of-a-kind pizza experience with our Avocado, Olives & Mushroom Pizza. Savor the versatility of avocado in every bite, complemented by the rich flavors of olives and mushrooms. It's a truly satisfying choice that you won't want to miss.

Makes: 1 Large Pizza
Baking Time: 15-20 minutes

Ingredients:
DOUGH
- ½ cup hot water
- 2 cups of baking mix with buttermilk

TOPPINGS
- A cup of tomato sauce, 8 ounces
- ½ cup of thinly sliced mushrooms
- ¼ cup finely minced green onion
- Two tablespoons of olive oil
- ⅓ cup of thinly sliced ripe olives
- ½ cup of mozzarella cheese, shredded
- 1 sliced tomato
- 1 sliced avocado
- Fresh leaves of basil

Instructions:
a) Set the oven for pizza to 425 °F.
b) Mix the buttermilk baking mix with boiling water.
c) Roll or pat the dough into a 12-inch circle and place it on a pizza pan or sheet pan.
d) Spread the tomato sauce and green onion mixture over the pizza dough.
e) Add mozzarella cheese, tomato slices, olives, and mushrooms on top.
f) Top with a drizzle of olive oil.
g) For 15 to 20 minutes, bake the crust's outer edge.
h) Take the pizza out of the oven and add avocado slices on top.
i) Add fresh basil leaves as a garnish when serving.

64) *Spinach and Ricotta Pizza*

Indulge in the comforting and classic flavors of Spinach and Ricotta Pizza. This variation boasts the creamy and delicate notes of ricotta cheese and sautéed spinach, making it a must-try for any pizza lover. Indulge in the ultimate pizza experience with our mouth-watering recipe. Savor the perfect combination of a crispy crust, zesty tomato sauce, sautéed spinach, velvety ricotta cheese, and a generous sprinkle of grated Parmesan. Indulge in the vibrant and earthy taste of our sautéed spinach, perfectly complemented by the luscious and creamy texture of our ricotta cheese. Indulge in the perfect blend of ingredients that come together to create a pizza that is not only satisfying but also bursting with wholesome flavors. Enhance the flavor profile of your dish by adding delectable toppings like zesty garlic, fiery red pepper flakes, or juicy sliced tomatoes. Indulge in the ultimate comfort food with our Spinach and Ricotta Pizza. Packed with nutritious veggies, this pizza is the perfect choice for those looking for a wholesome and satisfying meal.

Makes: 1 Large Pizza
Baking Time: 16 to 18 minutes

Ingredients:
- One traditional Italian basic dough recipe
- 3 minced garlic cloves
- six ounces of young spinach leaves
- 1½ ounces of finely grated Parmigiano
- ¼ teaspoon of ground nutmeg
- ¼ teaspoon of red pepper flakes
- ½ cup of white, dry wine
- Canola oil, 2 tablespoons
- ¼ cup ricotta
- Salt, ½ tea spoon
- One-half teaspoon of freshly cracked black pepper

Instructions:
a) Gently rotate and stretch the dough into a 14-inch-diameter circle.
b) Simmer the chopped garlic for 30 seconds in hot canola oil.
c) Add a drizzle of white wine and toss in the spices with the spinach.
d) Cook the spinach until it has wilted fully.
e) Continue by incorporating the ricotta, Parmigiano, salt, and black pepper.
f) Cover the crust with the spinach mixture.
g) For 16 to 18 minutes, bake or grill.

65) *Fig, taleggio and radicchio pizza*

Indulge in the ultimate pizza experience with our Fig, Taleggio, and Radicchio Pizza. This exquisite variation boasts a perfect balance of flavors, combining the luscious sweetness of figs, the velvety creaminess of Taleggio cheese, and the tantalizing bitterness of radicchio. Savor every bite of this sophisticated and flavor-packed pizza that is sure to leave your taste buds craving for more. Indulge in a mouth-watering pizza experience with our exquisite recipe. A delectable pizza crust is adorned with a luscious layer of fig jam or fresh figs, generously topped with slices of creamy Taleggio cheese, and finished off with thinly sliced radicchio. Savor every bite of this culinary masterpiece. Indulge in the exquisite combination of luscious figs and the decadent, nutty notes of Taleggio cheese. Experience a perfectly balanced pizza with the addition of radicchio, providing a delightful touch of bitterness to the overall flavor. Experience a truly unique and unforgettable pizza with our carefully crafted combination of premium ingredients. Elevate your taste experience with delectable toppings like caramelized onions, savory prosciutto, or a tantalizing drizzle of balsamic glaze. Indulge in the ultimate gourmet pizza experience with our Fig, Taleggio, and Radicchio Pizza. This sophisticated option boasts a perfect balance of sweet, creamy, and bitter flavors that will tantalize your taste buds.

Makes: 1 Large Pizza
Baking Time: 10-15 minutes

Ingredients:
- 6 oz. No-Knead Pizza Dough
- 3 dried figs from Mission
- 2 table spoons of chopped, roasted walnuts
- 12 head of shredded radicchio
- ½ cup dry red wine
- Extra-virgin olive oil, two tablespoons
- 2 ounces of chopped Taleggio cheese

Instructions:
a) Add the red wine to a medium-sized skillet with the dried figs and heat until boiling.
b) Turn off the heat and let the figs soak for at least 30 minutes.
c) After draining the figs, slice them into little pieces.
d) Spread 1 teaspoon of olive oil on the dough before topping it with Taleggio cheese, walnuts, radicchio, and figs.
e) For three to four minutes, broil.
f) Drizzle the remaining olive oil over the top.

66) *Marinara, arugula and lemon pizza*

Indulge in the perfect blend of simplicity and zest with our Marinara, Arugula, and Lemon Pizza. This refreshing and vibrant pizza variation boasts the peppery bite of arugula, the tanginess of lemon, and the classic simplicity of marinara sauce. Savor every bite of this deliciously unique pizza experience. Indulge in a mouthwatering pizza experience with our signature crust, smothered in a timeless marinara sauce, adorned with a bountiful serving of crisp arugula leaves, and finished off with a zesty lemon twist. Indulge in the rich and savory marinara sauce, perfectly complemented by the delightful freshness and subtle spiciness of arugula. Experience a burst of flavor with our zesty pizza, enhanced by the brightening touch of fresh lemon juice. Indulge in a pizza that is a perfect blend of lightness, tanginess, and an explosion of flavors, all thanks to the carefully selected ingredients. Indulge in the delightful Marinara, Arugula, and Lemon Pizza - a perfect pick for those seeking a pizza that's both uncomplicated and lively. This pizza celebrates the zesty tang of citrus and the crispness of greens, making for a truly refreshing experience.

Makes: 1 Large Pizza
Baking Time: 10-15 minutes

Ingredients:
- 1 Classic Italian Basic Dough
- One teaspoon of dried oregano
- Arugula, half a bunch
- ½ lemon
- Black pepper that's just been cracked
- Salt, ½ tea spoon
- 2 cups of pureed tomato
- One teaspoon of tomato paste
- ¼ teaspoon of red pepper flakes
- 2 cups of mozzarella cheese, shredded
- ½ cup grated Parmigiano-Reggiano
- 1 crushed garlic clove
- An olive oil drizzle

Instructions:
a) In a pan, reheat the tomato purée.
b) Include the tomato paste, dry oregano, and minced garlic. For 15 to 30 minutes, simmer.
c) Add salt, black pepper, and red pepper flakes for seasoning.
d) Take out the clove of garlic.
e) Use a rubber spatula to spread the sauce with a spoon into the center of the dough.
f) Sprinkle shredded mozzarella cheese over the sauce.
g) Bake in a 500°F pizza oven for roughly 15 minutes.
h) Sprinkle grated Parmigiano and arugula on top of the baked pizza.
i) Add a few drops of extra-virgin olive oil to the greens.

67) *Pesto Pizza*

Indulge in the timeless and delectable Pesto Pizza, a variation that highlights the fragrant and savory notes of pesto sauce. Indulge in a mouth-watering pizza experience with our signature recipe. Our crispy pizza crust is smothered with a luscious layer of aromatic basil pesto, topped with juicy sliced tomatoes, and generously sprinkled with premium mozzarella cheese. Experience a burst of fresh and fragrant flavors with our basil pesto, perfectly complemented by juicy and slightly tangy tomatoes. Experience the ultimate pizza indulgence with our perfectly melted mozzarella cheese that adds a creamy and luscious touch to every bite. Experience the vibrant and aromatic flavors of the Mediterranean with our expertly crafted pizza, made with a combination of carefully selected ingredients. Elevate your taste experience by adding delectable toppings like pine nuts, Parmesan cheese, or fresh basil leaves to your dish. Indulge in the exquisite flavors of Pesto Pizza - a perfect pick for those craving a burst of herbal goodness and a taste of authentic Italian-inspired delight.

Makes: 1 Large Pizza
Baking Time: 10-15 minutes

Ingredients:
- 12-inch dough shell in the New York style
- Two cups of finely shredded mozzarella cheese
- 1 and a half cups of spinach leaves
- ½ cup basil leaves
- 1 ½ table spoons of olive oil
- 1 clove of garlic
- 1 cup of finely chopped Parmesan cheese
- Oil of olives
- ⅓ cup of sliced, drained sun-dried tomatoes

Instructions:
a) In a food processor, combine spinach, basil, olive oil, and garlic.
b) Preheat the oven for pizza at 500°F.
c) Apply olive oil to a 12-inch pizza pan.
d) Spread the dough evenly throughout the pan and top with all of the pesto.
e) Top the pesto with the sun-dried tomatoes.
f) Top the pizza with the grated mozzarella cheese.
g) Bake the pizza at 450 degrees for 15 minutes, or until the dough has golden.

68) *Mixed Veggie Pizza*

Indulge in the vibrant and nourishing Mixed Veggie Pizza, a delectable variation that pays homage to the bounty of seasonal vegetables. Indulge in a mouthwatering pizza experience with our latest recipe. Our signature pizza crust is adorned with a colorful assortment of crisp and succulent vegetables, including bell peppers, mushrooms, zucchini, and onions. Experience a feast for your eyes and taste buds with our expertly crafted pizza. Our vegetables are sliced to perfection and artfully arranged on top, resulting in a stunning and delicious combination that will leave you wanting more. Elevate your pizza experience with the perfect combination of tangy tomato sauce, melted cheese, and a tantalizing blend of herbs and spices. Indulge in a nutrient-rich pizza that boasts a vibrant array of colors and highlights the natural flavors of fresh vegetables. Indulge in the goodness of a Mixed Veggie Pizza that promises a veggie-forward and nutritious pizza experience. Satisfy your cravings with a delicious and wholesome treat that is sure to leave you feeling content.

Makes: 1 Large Pizza
Baking Time: about 10 minutes

Ingredients:
- One whole wheat pizza crust
- Pizza sauce, 1 cup
- 12 ounces of vegetables, mixed
- 1 ounce of thinly sliced pepperoni
- One tablespoon of olive oil
- 1 cup of mozzarella cheese, shredded

Instructions:
a) Set your pizza oven's temperature to 450 degrees.
b) In a skillet with hot olive oil, sauté the mixed vegetables for 10 minutes.
c) Place the mozzarella cheese, pepperoni, and veggie mixture on top of the pizza sauce-covered crust.
d) Bake for about 10 minutes in the oven.

69) *Four Cheese Pizza/Quattro formaggi*

Indulge in the heavenly richness of Quattro Formaggi, also known as Four Cheese Pizza. This delectable pizza variation is a cheese lover's dream come true, featuring a blend of multiple cheeses that will leave your taste buds in pure bliss. Indulge in the ultimate cheesy goodness with our four-cheese pizza recipe! Our mouth-watering pizza crust is generously topped with a delectable blend of premium mozzarella, Parmesan, Gorgonzola, and Fontina cheeses. Indulge in a harmonious blend of flavors with this exquisite cheese combination. The stretchy and melty texture of mozzarella, the nutty and salty taste of Parmesan, the creamy and tangy bite of Gorgonzola, and the mild and buttery note of Fontina come together to create a symphony of taste that will leave your palate singing. Indulge in the ultimate pizza experience with our decadent, creamy, and irresistibly cheesy masterpiece. Enhance the already delicious flavors of the cheeses by adding some fresh herbs or a drizzle of honey as toppings. Indulge in the ultimate pizza experience with our Four Cheese Pizza/Quattro Formaggi. Perfect for cheese lovers, this pizza is a truly unforgettable choice that will leave your taste buds craving more.

Makes: 1 Large Pizza
Baking Time: 16 to 18 minutes

Ingredients:

- 4 oz. of grated mozzarella cheese
- One traditional Italian basic dough recipe
- Roasted garlic, 1 head
- One teaspoon of Dijon mustard
- 4 ounces of provolone cheese, shredded
- 2 tea spoons of freshly ground black pepper
- 2 ounces of Pecorino cheese, finely grated
- One tablespoon of olive oil
- 4 ounces of finely chopped Muenster cheese
- 2 teaspoons of freshly grated nutmeg

Instructions:

a) Shape the dough into a 14-inch-diameter circle.
b) Do this by holding the edges and carefully rotating and stretching the dough.
c) Blend the roasted garlic cloves with the olive oil and Dijon mustard.
d) Distribute this mixture over the crust evenly.
e) After mixing all the cheeses, sprinkle them over the crust.
f) Season with nutmeg and black pepper.
g) For 16 to 18 minutes, grill or bake.

70) *Melanzane Pizza*

Experience the delicious and unique flavor of Melanzane Pizza, also known as Eggplant Pizza. This delightful pizza variation showcases the meaty and tender texture of eggplant, making it a truly satisfying and enjoyable meal. Indulge in a mouth-watering pizza experience with our delectable recipe. Our signature pizza crust is adorned with succulent slices of roasted or grilled eggplant, tangy tomato sauce, and a generous layer of creamy mozzarella cheese. A sprinkle of fragrant herbs adds the perfect finishing touch to this irresistible dish. Indulge in the mouth-watering goodness of our pizza topped with succulent eggplant that is cooked to perfection, delivering a burst of flavors with every bite. Indulge in the rich and tangy flavor of our tomato sauce, perfectly complemented by the creamy and melty goodness of our mozzarella cheese. Indulge in a hearty and flavorful Mediterranean pizza that's a vegetable enthusiast's dream come true, thanks to the perfect combination of carefully selected ingredients. Enhance the overall flavor by adding premium toppings like fresh basil, olives, or a delectable drizzle of olive oil. Indulge in the delectable Melanzane Pizza, perfect for those seeking to savor the distinct flavor and texture of eggplant in their pizza.

Makes: 1 Large Pizza
Baking Time: 16 to 18 minutes

Ingredients:
- One traditional Italian basic dough recipe
- Olive oil, ¼ cup
- 1 cup of white wine that is dry
- 4 chopped garlic cloves
- 2 tea spoons of oregano leaves, chopped
- Salt, ½ tea spoon
- One-half teaspoon of freshly cracked black pepper
- Pizza sauce, 1 cup
- One-half teaspoon of freshly cracked black pepper
- A single eggplant, cut into strips.
- 1 cup of room temperature ricotta
- One ounce of grated Pecorino, Grana Padano, or Parmigiano cheese
- 4 oz. of grated mozzarella cheese

Instructions:
a) Holding the edges, carefully rotate and stretch the dough into a circle with a 14-inch diameter.
b) In a skillet with hot oil, add the eggplant strips and cook for 5 minutes.
c) Cook for three more minutes in the skillet after adding the minced garlic, oregano, salt, and black pepper.
d) Place the pizza sauce on top of the prepared crust.
e) Cover the sauce with the cooked eggplant mixture.
f) Combine the ricotta and the shredded cheese, then top the pizza with it.
g) For 16 to 18 minutes, grill or bake.

71) *Raclette Pizza*

Experience a delightful twist on the classic pizza with Raclette Pizza. Savor the mouthwatering goodness of melted raclette cheese that takes your taste buds on a delectable journey. Indulge in a mouthwatering pizza experience with our signature recipe. Our delectable crust is smothered with a lavish layer of raclette cheese, complemented by a medley of cured meats, tangy pickles, and savory potatoes. Savor every bite of this irresistible masterpiece. Indulge in the smooth and creamy texture of raclette cheese as it melts beautifully over our pizza, creating a gooey and irresistible experience. Indulge in the delectable blend of melted cheese, savory meats, tangy pickles, and hearty potatoes for a flavor profile that is both rich and balanced. Satisfy your cravings with every bite. Indulge in the ultimate cheesy delight with Raclette Pizza - a true masterpiece for cheese aficionados and pizza enthusiasts alike. Savor the distinct and delectable flavor of raclette cheese, perfectly crafted to elevate your pizza experience to new heights.

Makes: 1 Large Pizza
Baking Time: 16 to 18 minutes

Ingredients:
- One traditional Italian basic dough recipe
- 8 ounces of finely chopped Raclette
- two tablespoons of Dijon mustard
- ¾ pound of cooked and peeled Yukon gold potatoes
- ½ cup of cornichons, chopped

Instructions:
a) Holding the edges, carefully rotate and stretch the dough into a circle with a 14-inch diameter.
b) Cover the crust with a thin layer of Dijon mustard.
c) Top with the shredded Raclette.
d) Arrange the cheese on top of the hot potatoes, then top with the cornichons.
e) For 16 to 18 minutes, grill or bake.

72) *Ratatouille Pizza*

Indulge in the delectable Ratatouille Pizza, a vegetable-centric and savory pizza rendition that draws inspiration from the timeless French delicacy. Indulge in a mouth-watering pizza experience with our delectable recipe. Our signature pizza crust is adorned with a delightful medley of sautéed vegetables, including eggplant, zucchini, bell peppers, and tomatoes. The aromatic herbs of thyme and oregano add a burst of flavor to this savory masterpiece. Experience the perfect blend of tender and fragrant vegetables on our pizza, as their natural flavors infuse every bite. The harmonious combination of textures will leave your taste buds craving for more. Experience a burst of freshness and complexity in every bite with the addition of our carefully selected herbs. Indulge in the delightful Ratatouille Pizza, a perfect pick for those who crave a healthier and more nourishing pizza indulgence. This pizza is a true celebration of the rich and lively flavors of Mediterranean veggies.

Makes: 1 Large Pizza
Baking Time: 19 minutes

Ingredients:
- One traditional Italian basic dough recipe
- One-half teaspoon of red pepper flakes
- 1 chopped tomato
- One tablespoon of thyme leaves
- 1 chopped shallot
- 1 sliced garlic clove
- 1 cup of peeled and diced eggplant
- One-half teaspoon of freshly cracked black pepper
- Two tablespoons of olive oil
- 1 chopped green bell pepper
- 1 teaspoon of fresh rosemary
- Salt, ½ tea spoon
- 6 ounces of finely chopped Gruyère
- 1½ ounces of finely grated Parmigiano

Instructions:
a) Holding the edges, carefully rotate and stretch the dough into a circle with a 14-inch diameter.
b) In a skillet over medium heat, add the garlic and shallot. Cook, turning often, for 2 minutes.
c) Add the salt, rosemary, black pepper, green bell pepper, tomato, eggplant, and other seasonings.
d) Boil for approximately 30 minutes.
e) Sprinkle the shredded Gruyère evenly over the crust.
f) Evenly distribute the eggplant mixture over the cheese.
g) Top with some Parmigiano cheese.
h) 19 minutes in the oven.

73) *Stir-Fry Pizza*

Indulge in the delectable fusion of Italian and Asian cuisine with Stir-Fry Pizza. This unique dish combines the classic flavors of pizza with the bold and savory notes of stir-fried dishes, resulting in a truly unforgettable culinary experience. Indulge in a mouthwatering pizza crust that is generously topped with a delectable stir-fry of fresh vegetables, your choice of protein (chicken, beef, or tofu), and a tantalizing sauce that is sure to leave your taste buds craving for more. Experience the perfect stir-fry every time with our expertly cooked ingredients that are tender-crisp, preserving their natural freshness and texture. Experience a burst of savory and umami-rich flavors as the sauce seamlessly ties all the ingredients together. Experience a mouthwatering fusion of textures and flavors with Stir-Fry Pizza. Our crispy crust provides the perfect foundation for our succulent stir-fried toppings, creating a truly delightful culinary experience. Experience a world of bold and innovative pizza flavors with this fantastic choice.

Makes: 1 Large Pizza
Baking Time: 18 minutes

Ingredients:
- 1½ table spoons of soy sauce
- One traditional Italian basic dough recipe
- 8 ounces of matchstick-sized pork loin
- One tablespoon of rice vinegar
- 4 ounces of soy mozzarella cheese, grated
- 2 cups of mixed, finely chopped quick-cooking vegetables.
- 6 table spoons of dark Chinese dipping sauce
- Sesame oil, two tablespoons
- One tablespoon of sesame seeds

Instructions:
a) Holding the edges, carefully rotate and stretch the dough into a circle with a 14-inch diameter.
b) Combine the pork with one tablespoon of soy sauce and rice vinegar.
c) Cook the pork for two to three minutes in a skillet that has been heated with a tablespoon of sesame oil.
d) Spread the crust with the black Chinese seasoning sauce.
e) Top with soy cheese that has been shred.
f) Top the pizza with the cooked meat and finely chopped veggies.
g) Top the crust with the remaining tablespoon of sesame oil and sesame seeds.
h) 18 to 20 minutes of baking.

74) *Mini Portobello pizzas*

Introducing the Mini Portobello Pizzas - a delightful and compact take on the timeless pizza. Indulge in a unique twist on traditional pizza with our mouth-watering recipe. Our savory portobello mushroom caps serve as the perfect foundation for a delectable medley of toppings, including rich tomato sauce, gooey cheese, and all your favorite fixings. Indulge in the rich and hearty texture of portobello mushrooms, delivering a truly satisfying bite. Experience the classic taste of pizza with our signature tomato sauce and cheese. Elevate your taste buds with our selection of premium toppings that perfectly complement the rich flavors of our pizza. Indulge in the mouth-watering flavor of Mini Portobello Pizzas, a perfect choice for those who prefer a healthier and gluten-free option over the conventional pizza crust. Indulge in the delectable goodness of these savory treats that can be relished as a delightful appetizer, a scrumptious snack, or a satisfying main course for those who adore mushrooms.

Makes: 4
Baking Time: 9 minutes

Ingredients:
- 20 pepperoni slices
- 1 thinly sliced vine tomato
- ¼ cup finely chopped fresh basil
- A dash of pepper and low-sodium salt
- Cheese, 4 ounces
- Four Portobello mushroom caps with their interiors scraped out
- Olive oil, six table spoons

Instructions
a) Rub a little olive oil and salt and pepper on the mushrooms' undersides.
b) 7 minutes of broiling the mushrooms.
c) Place a basil leaf and a tomato slice inside each mushroom.
d) Top each mushroom with five slices of pepperoni and cheese.
e) Broil for two more minutes.

75) *Chanterelle Pizza with Cheese*

Indulge in the exquisite taste of Chanterelle Pizza with Cheese, a gourmet variation that highlights the subtle and earthy notes of chanterelle mushrooms. Indulge in a gourmet pizza experience with our delectable recipe. Savor the earthy flavors of sautéed chanterelle mushrooms, perfectly paired with a blend of premium cheeses such as Gruyere or Fontina. Infused with aromatic fresh herbs and garlic, this pizza is a true masterpiece. Indulge in the exquisite taste and hearty texture of chanterelle mushrooms, the perfect addition to elevate your pizza experience. Experience the ultimate indulgence with our exquisite blend of cheeses. The creamy texture and rich flavor will tantalize your taste buds, while the infusion of herbs and garlic will elevate your culinary experience to new heights. Indulge in the exquisite Chanterelle Pizza with Cheese, a must-try for mushroom aficionados and pizza connoisseurs seeking a refined and upscale dining experience.

Makes: 2 pizzas
Baking Time: 10-15 minutes

Ingredients:

- Two typical pizza dough recipes
- 3 cups of chanterelles, sliced in half and rinsed
- Salt, ¼ tea spoon
- Fresh oregano, 1 tablespoon
- One dash of garlic powder
- Cheddar Sauce
- ½ cup tomato puree
- 1 teaspoon of fresh basil

Instructions

a) Set the pizza oven's temperature to 480°F.
b) Holding the dough's edges, carefully rotate and stretch the dough into two 14-inch-diameter rings.
c) Combine the tomato purée, salt, and garlic powder.
d) Apply the cheese sauce and the combination to the dough.
e) After 10 to 15 minutes of baking, top the pizza with the chanterelles.
f) After baking, top with fresh basil and oregano.

76) *Mushroom & Shallot White Pizza*

Indulge in the savory and delectable Mushroom & Shallot White Pizza, a unique take on the classic pizza. This culinary masterpiece boasts a luscious and rich white sauce that is sure to tantalize your taste buds. Indulge in a mouthwatering pizza experience with our signature crust, smothered in a luscious white sauce, adorned with sautéed mushrooms and caramelized shallots, and finished off with a tantalizing blend of herbs and cheese. Indulge in the rich and savory foundation of toppings with our luscious white sauce, crafted with premium ingredients such as cream, garlic, and Parmesan cheese. Indulge in the rich and earthy flavor of sautéed mushrooms, perfectly complemented by the sweet and deep notes of caramelized shallots. Indulge in the ultimate pizza experience with our rich, aromatic, and umami-packed combination of ingredients. Indulge in a luxurious pizza experience with our Mushroom & Shallot White Pizza. This delectable choice is perfect for those seeking to explore a unique flavor profile.

Makes: 4
Baking Time: 10 minutes

Ingredients:
- 1 basic Italian dough
- 4 sliced and stemmed shiitake mushrooms
- 1 tea spoon chopped fresh thyme
- 1 sliced shallot
- Sun-dried tomato oil, three tablespoons
- ¼ cup of chopped, oil-drained sun-dried tomatoes
- 4 teaspoons of cream cheese
- 1 smashed garlic clove
- Pepper and salt
- 3 teaspoons of creamer

TO SERVE
- Arugula
- Drizzling olive oil
- Fresh Basil
- 1 dash of red pepper flakes

Instructions
a) Fry the shallots and mushrooms in the sun-dried tomato oil.
b) Add salt and pepper to taste.
c) Combine the remaining 2 table spoons of oil with the thyme, basil, and garlic in a different bowl. Place aside.
d) In another bowl, mix together the cream cheese and creamer. Place aside.
e) Spread the dough on a sheet pan that has been greased.
f) Cover the dough with the oil and herb mixture.
g) Top with the sun-dried tomatoes.
h) Smother the tomatoes with the cream cheese mixture.
i) Sprinkle the top with the mushrooms and shallots.
j) Bake for 10 minutes, then garnish with fresh basil, arugula, red pepper flakes, and a drizzle of olive oil before serving.

77) *Bean Nacho Pizza*

Indulge in the ultimate culinary delight with our Bean Nacho Pizza - a delectable fusion of pizza and nachos that will tantalize your taste buds. Experience the perfect blend of two classic dishes, crafted to perfection for your ultimate satisfaction. Indulge in a mouthwatering pizza crust that's layered with savory refried beans, gooey melted cheese, and a medley of toppings that will transport you to the nostalgic flavors of classic nachos. Savor the burst of flavors from the diced tomatoes, jalapeños, olives, and a dollop of sour cream that will leave your taste buds craving for more. Indulge in the rich and velvety flavor of refried beans, perfectly complemented by the luscious and melted cheese that creates a tantalizingly gooey texture. Experience a burst of flavors with our delicious toppings that offer the perfect balance of heat, tanginess, and freshness. Indulge in the ultimate pizza experience with our Bean Nacho Pizza! This playful and exciting pizza combines the classic comfort of pizza with the bold and vibrant flavors of nachos. Satisfy your cravings and treat your taste buds to a truly unique and delicious pizza adventure.

Makes: 1
Baking Time: 15-18 minutes

Ingredients:
- One traditional Italian basic dough recipe
- Salt, ½ tea spoon
- 6 ounces of cheese, grated
- 3 chopped plum tomatoes
- Slices of pickled jalapenos in a jar.
- 1¼ cups of refried beans in a can.
- One-half teaspoon of ground cumin
- One-half teaspoon of freshly cracked black pepper
- 1 tea spoon of finely chopped oregano
- ⅓ cup salsa

Instructions:
a)   Roll the dough into a circle with a diameter of 14 inches and place it on a pizza peel or sheet pan.
b)   Sprinkle cheese and refried beans on top of the crust.
c)   Add salt, black pepper, oregano, cumin, and other seasonings.
d)   Top the pizza dough with salsa.
e)   Grill the pizza or bake it for 15 to 18 minutes.
f)   Before cutting and serving the pizza, top it with slices of jalapeno.

78) *Lemon Roasted Broccoli Whole Wheat Pizza*

Indulge in the wholesome and nutritious Lemon Roasted Broccoli Whole Wheat Pizza, a delectable variation that boasts the vibrant flavors of roasted broccoli and the nuttiness of whole wheat crust. Indulge in a wholesome pizza experience with our signature whole wheat crust recipe. Topped with oven-roasted broccoli florets, a zesty squeeze of fresh lemon juice, and a generous sprinkle of Parmesan cheese, this pizza is a true delight for your taste buds. Customize it with your favorite toppings like red pepper flakes or garlic for an added kick of flavor. Indulge in the irresistible texture and subtle sweetness of our roasted broccoli, perfectly caramelized to perfection. Experience a burst of brightness and tanginess with the addition of fresh lemon juice, perfectly balancing the richness of the cheese. Indulge in the rich and wholesome flavor of our whole wheat crust, boasting a nutty and hearty taste that elevates the overall flavor profile to new heights. Indulge in the delectable Lemon Roasted Broccoli Whole Wheat Pizza, a perfect pick for those who crave a healthier pizza alternative without sacrificing on flavor or consistency.

Makes: 1
Baking Time: 10-15 minutes

Ingredients:
- One whole-wheat pizza dough recipe
- One teaspoon of red pepper flakes
- ½ a sliced lemon
- ¼ cup of cheese crumbles
- ¼ cup basil pesto
- 1-half lemon zest

- Sun-dried tomato chunks in the amount of ¼ cup
- 2 cups of finely minced broccoli florets
- One-quarter cup of chopped Kalamata olives
- Fresh cheese weighing 8 ounces
- ½ cup of microgreen mustard

Instructions:
a) Set the oven for pizza to 425 °F.
b) Roll the dough out to an extremely thin thickness.
c) Set the dough on a sheet pan that has been lined.
d) Cover the dough with pesto.
e) Sprinkle the top with the cheese crumbles, sun-dried tomatoes, olives, lemon zest, and red pepper flakes.
f) Place the broccoli and 1 tablespoon of sun-dried tomato oil in a bowl.
g) Top with the broccoli and wedges of lemon.
h) Bake anything for 10–15 minutes.
i) Take the pizza out of the oven.

79) *Mixed Microgreens Pizza*

Indulge in the refreshing and vibrant flavors of microgreens with our Mixed Microgreens Pizza. This pizza variation is a celebration of delicate and exquisite flavors that will tantalize your taste buds. Indulge in a delectable pizza crust that's adorned with a medley of mixed microgreens, including the likes of baby arugula, watercress, and radish sprouts. Experience a burst of freshness with these tiny greens that offer a delightful crunch and a range of flavors from peppery to slightly tangy. Elevate your Mixed Microgreens Pizza experience with a tantalizing drizzle of premium olive oil, a delicate sprinkle of exquisite sea salt, or a generous shaving of delectable Parmesan cheese. Your taste buds will thank you. Indulge in a feast for both your eyes and taste buds with our visually stunning pizza that packs a punch of nutrient-rich greens. Indulge in a delightful pizza experience that perfectly captures the essence of microgreens. Our light and refreshing pizza is the ultimate choice for those seeking a truly exquisite taste.

Makes: 1
Baking Time: 12-15 minutes

Ingredients:
- 1 Classic Italian Basic Dough
- 1 dash of seasoned salt
- 1 dash of garlic salt
- 1 dash of red pepper flakes
- 1 cup of microgreens in a spicy mix
- One teaspoon of olive oil
- Cheddar
- ½ lemon

Instructions:
a) Arrange the pizza dough in layers on a sheet pan with foil.
b) Season the dough with Italian seasoning, garlic salt, and red pepper flakes.
c) Sprinkle cheese on top, then bake for 12 to 15 minutes at 500 °F.
d) Combine the microgreens with some salt, lemon juice, and olive oil in a bowl.
e) After taking the pizza out of the oven, plate it and add some dressed microgreens on top.

80) *Spring Greens Pizza*

Indulge in the delectable Spring Greens Pizza, a true celebration of the lively and fresh flavors of the season. Indulge in the freshness of spring with our delectable pizza recipe. A crispy crust serves as the perfect base for a medley of vibrant greens, including baby spinach, tender asparagus spears, and sweet peas. For an extra burst of flavor, we recommend adding some fragrant herbs like mint or basil. Experience the freshness of spring with our delicious pizza topped with crisp and lively greens. Enjoy a perfect combination of textures and a range of flavors, from earthy to slightly sweet, that will tantalize your taste buds. Elevate your pizza experience with a delicate sauce, a touch of cheese, or a tantalizing balsamic glaze. Indulge in the ultimate pizza experience that celebrates the bountiful freshness of spring produce with Spring Greens Pizza. This delectable dish is the perfect choice to savor during the season's peak, offering a burst of flavor and a refreshing twist to your taste buds.

Makes: 2
Baking Time: 15-20 minutes

Ingredients:
- Extra virgin olive oil, ¼ cup
- Whole Wheat Pizza Dough, 1 recipe
- 8 ounces of sliced and divided fresh mozzarella cheese
- Two cups of young arugula
- Two tablespoons of white wine vinegar
- One-fourth teaspoon kosher salt
- Black pepper, cracked
- One cup of young spinach
- ½ cup of microgreens in a spicy mix
- ¼ cup of cherry tomatoes, sliced
- ¾ of a tea spoon of Dijon mustard
- ¼ cup of parmesan cheese, shaved
- Fresh basil, for decoration

Instructions:
a) Set the oven for pizza to 425 °F.
b) On a lightly dusted surface, cut out two 8-inch circles from the dough.
c) Place the dough on a baking sheet.
d) Top each piece of dough with 4 ounces of cheese.
e) The pizza should be baked for 15 to 20 minutes.
f) Combine the mustard, vinegar, oil, salt, and pepper in a basin.
g) Combine the vinaigrette with the arugula, spinach, and microgreens.
h) Place the greens mixture and cherry tomatoes on each pizza.
i) Add shaved parmesan cheese on top and garnish with fresh basil.

81) *Flatbread with Arugula Microgreens*

Indulge in the exquisite taste of our Flatbread with Arugula Microgreens - a delightful appetizer or light meal that perfectly highlights the vibrant flavors and delicate textures of arugula microgreens. Indulge in a delectable culinary experience with our signature recipe that boasts a thin and crispy flatbread as the foundation, adorned with an ample serving of freshly-picked arugula microgreens. Experience the bold and zesty flavors of our microgreens, harvested at the peak of freshness for a concentrated burst of taste. With their delightful crunch and tangy notes, these greens are the perfect addition to any dish. Elevate the taste of your flatbread with a drizzle of premium olive oil, a sprinkle of exquisite sea salt, or even some finely shaved Parmesan cheese. Indulge in the delicate and refreshing flavors of microgreens with our Flatbread with Arugula Microgreens. This dish is a perfect choice for those who appreciate the beauty and taste of microgreens in a simple yet delightful way.

Makes: 1
Baking Time: 4 minutes

Ingredients:

- 1 basic Italian dough
- ¼ cup pesto
- One cup of quartered cherry tomatoes
- A half apple, sliced into matchsticks.
- 1 chopped avocado

- 2 cups of microgreen arugula
- One-half teaspoon olive oil
- Shredded cheese
- Lemon juice, ½ cup
- Pepper and salt

Instructions:

a) Turn the oven's temperature up to 550 degrees.
b) Lightly cook the pizza dough in the oven for a little period of time.
c) Take the crust out of the oven and top it with pesto.
d) Combine the apple, avocado, cherry tomatoes, and microgreen arugula in a bowl.
e) Add salt, pepper, lemon juice, and olive oil to the mixture as seasonings. Add some shaved cheese.
f) Top the flatbread crust with the mixture.
g) Sliced food is served.

82) *Mild Microgreen Forest Pizza*

Introducing the Mild Microgreen Forest Pizza - a one-of-a-kind culinary masterpiece that is as visually stunning as it is delicious. This pizza creation boasts a variety of mild-flavored microgreens, arranged to resemble a lush forest atop a perfectly baked crust. Indulge in a delectable pizza crust that is adorned with a delightful blend of gentle microgreens, including pea shoots, sunflower sprouts, and baby lettuces. Experience the delicate and tender texture of our microgreens, paired with their mild flavors to create a harmonious and refreshing taste profile. Elevate your pizza experience with our customizable options. Opt for a light sauce, a sprinkle of cheese, or indulge in additional toppings such as cherry tomatoes or avocado slices. Indulge in the exquisite Mild Microgreen Forest Pizza - a visual and culinary masterpiece that celebrates the stunning allure and delectable taste of microgreens. This pizza is the perfect choice for those who crave a one-of-a-kind and lively pizza adventure.

Makes: 1 Large Pizza
Baking Time: 6-9 minutes

Ingredients:
- 1 Classic Italian Basic Dough
- ½ cup of chile-based sauce
- ½ cup of frozen fresh cheese that has been grated.
- 4 ounces of cremini mushrooms, sliced
- 2 ounces of broccolini
- 1 and a half cups of arugula
- ⅓ cup of shaved cheese
- Mild mix microgreens

Instructions:
a) Coat a pizza peel with cornmeal or semolina flour and set it aside.
b) Position the pizza stone in the bottom third of your oven and preheat it to 500 degrees.
c) Transfer the pizza dough to a surface dusted with flour.
d) Stretch the dough into the shape of a pizza, leaving a crust edge or rim.
e) Spoon the chimichurri evenly across the center of the pizza.
f) Sprinkle most of the grated cheese on top.
g) Arrange the sliced cremini mushrooms and broccolini florets on top.
h) Bake the pizza for 6 to 9 minutes.
i) About halfway through baking, turn the pizza to ensure even cooking.
j) Remove from the oven and slice.
k) Top the pizza with arugula, additional shaved cheese, black pepper, and microgreens.

83) *Nduja Pizza with Basil*

Indulge in the fiery and bold flavors of our Nduja Pizza with Basil. This pizza variation features the intense and spicy taste of nduja, a spreadable Calabrian salami, perfectly complemented by the freshness of basil. Satisfy your cravings with this daring and flavorful pizza today. Indulge in the ultimate pizza experience with our mouth-watering recipe. Our signature pizza crust is generously topped with a delectable spread of nduja, infusing every bite with its rich, smoky, and spicy flavors. Experience a tantalizing flavor sensation that is sure to delight your adventurous palate with the addition of nduja. Its depth of heat and umami will elevate your taste buds to new heights. Experience the perfect balance of flavors with our delicious pizza. The spiciness of the nduja is perfectly complemented by the cool and refreshing notes of fresh basil leaves. Indulge in a pizza experience like no other with our Nduja Pizza featuring the perfect blend of bold and unique flavors. The fiery heat of the nduja is perfectly complemented by the bright and aromatic notes of basil, making it a truly unforgettable choice for pizza lovers.

Makes: 1 large pizza
Baking Time: 10-15 minutes

Ingredients
- 1 recipe of Traditional Italian basic Dough
- 2 table spoons grated Parmigiano Reggiano
- 1 ball of Burrata cheese
- 2 table spoons Nduja
- 4.4 ounces of fresh mozzarella
- ¼ cup of tomato passata
- ¼ tea spoon dried oregano
- One teaspoon of olive oil
- 1 handful fresh basil

Instructions
a) Preheat the pizza oven to 535°F or the maximum setting.
b) Sprinkle some flour or semolina on your pizza pan.
c) Roll out half of the dough and fit it into the tray by rolling it out to fit.
d) In a small bowl, mix the tomato passata, olive oil, and dried oregano.
e) Spread the passata mixture evenly on the pizza dough.
f) Top with fresh mozzarella and spoonfuls of Nduja.
g) Bake the pizza for 10-15 minutes in the oven.
h) Once cooked, top with grated Parmigiano Reggiano and pieces of Burrata cheese.
i) Sprinkle fresh basil on top and serve.

84) *Sicilian Pizza/ Sfincione*

Indulge in the timeless and adored Sicilian Pizza, also referred to as Sfincione, hailing from the picturesque region of Sicily, Italy. Indulge in the ultimate pizza experience with our signature recipe. Savor the thick and fluffy rectangular crust, perfectly complemented by a flavorful tomato sauce, onions, anchovies, and a generous amount of grated caciocavallo or pecorino cheese. Indulge in a mouthwatering pizza that's been expertly baked to perfection. Savor the hearty and satisfying dish that boasts a delectable interplay of flavors. Indulge in the delectable flavors of our tomato sauce, boasting a perfect balance of sweet and tangy notes. The savory and slightly sweet addition of onions elevates the taste to new heights. Experience a subtle brininess and depth in every bite with the addition of anchovies, elevating the overall taste profile to new heights. Indulge in a mouthwatering experience with our grated cheese, which adds a luscious and velvety texture to every morsel. Indulge in the Sicilian Pizza/Sfincione for a truly authentic taste of Sicily. With its one-of-a-kind crust and delectable toppings that have withstood the test of time, this pizza is a must-try for those seeking a distinctive culinary experience.

Makes: 16 thick slices
Baking Time: 25-30 minutes

Ingredients
- 2 recipes of Traditional Italian basic Dough
- 2 portions of pizza sauce

TOPPING
- 1 tea spoon olive oil
- ¼ cup of breadcrumbs
- ¼ cup of grated pecorino or parmesan
- 1 tea spoon dried oregano

Instructions
a) Preheat the pizza oven to 450°F/230°C.
b) On a lightly floured surface, spread out each portion of the dough and divide it in half.
c) Form each half into a circle.
d) Lightly brush a sheet pan with olive oil and transfer the dough onto it.
e) Spoon half of the prepared pizza sauce over each pizza dough.
f) Sprinkle breadcrumbs, grated pecorino or parmesan, dried oregano, and olive oil evenly over each pizza.
g) Bake the pizzas for 25 to 30 minutes or until golden and cooked through.

CHAPTER 6: FRUIT PIZZA

85) *Sweet and spicy pineapple pizza*

Indulge in the perfect balance of sweet and spicy with our mouth-watering Sweet and Spicy Pineapple Pizza. This delectable fusion of flavors combines the juicy sweetness of pineapple with a tantalizing hint of spiciness, resulting in a truly unique and unforgettable pizza experience. Indulge in a mouthwatering pizza experience with our signature recipe. Our crispy pizza crust is smothered with a tangy tomato sauce, generously topped with premium mozzarella cheese, and finished off with succulent pineapple chunks. Experience the perfect balance of sweet and spicy with our expertly crafted recipe. We've added just the right amount of jalapeños or red pepper flakes to provide a subtle kick that tantalizes your taste buds and perfectly complements the sweetness of our juicy pineapple. Experience a tantalizing burst of flavors with our signature dish featuring juicy pineapple, gooey melted cheese, and a spicy kick that will leave your taste buds craving for more. Indulge in the tantalizing flavors of our Sweet and Spicy Pineapple Pizza! This delightful creation is perfect for those who crave a fun and daring twist on the classic pizza, complete with a touch of the tropics.

Makes: 1
Baking Time: 10-15 minutes

Ingredients:
- 1 recipe No-Knead Bread and Pizza Dough
- ½ cup Chipotle Salsa
- ¼ cup Fresh cilantro or basil, chopped
- 1 cup Shredded cheese
- Extra-virgin olive oil, for greasing
- 1 cup Baby arugula
- 1 cup Fresh pineapple chunks
- 2 green onions, chopped

Instructions:
a) Turn the pizza oven on at 450 degrees Fahrenheit.
b) On a surface that has been lightly sprinkled with flour, roll out the dough to a thickness of 1/4 inch.
c) Gently place the dough on a sheet pan that has been oiled or lined.
d) Cover the dough with the chipotle salsa.
e) Top the salsa with shredded cheese, then scatter chopped cilantro or basil and pineapple chunks over top.
f) Put the pizza in the oven for 10 to 15 minutes.
g) Add green onions and baby arugula as a garnish.

86) *BBQ Strawberry Pizza*

Indulge in the delectable BBQ Strawberry Pizza, a one-of-a-kind culinary creation that expertly blends the rich, smoky notes of barbecue sauce with the luscious sweetness of freshly-picked strawberries. Indulge in a mouthwatering pizza experience with our signature recipe. Our delectable crust is generously layered with tangy barbecue sauce, succulent chicken or pork, juicy sliced strawberries, and a sprinkle of cheese to top it off. Savor every bite of this irresistible combination. Experience the perfect harmony of flavors with our savory barbecue sauce and juicy strawberries. The sweetness of the fruit perfectly complements the rich and tangy barbecue sauce, creating a truly delicious taste sensation. Elevate your dish with the protein-packed goodness and smoky flavor of chicken or pork. The perfect complement to the fruity sweetness you crave. Indulge in the delectable BBQ Strawberry Pizza, perfect for the adventurous foodies who crave the tantalizing blend of savory and sweet flavors in their pizza.

Makes: 1
Baking Time: about 15 minutes

Ingredients:
- 1 Traditional Italian basic Dough
- 1 cup Boursin cheese
- Shaved parmesan, for garnish
- 2 cups Sliced strawberries
- ⅓ cup Chopped basil
- 1 pinch Pepper
- 2 tablespoons Balsamic glaze
- 1 tablespoon Olive oil

Instructions:
a) Place the pizza crust on a grill or bake it in an oven.
b) After removing from the oven, sprinkle Boursin cheese on top.
c) Add chopped basil and strawberry slices as a garnish.
d) Add pepper and parmesan shavings as a garnish.
e) Drizzle with balsamic glaze and olive oil.

87) *Cherry Almond Pizza*

Indulge in the delectable Cherry Almond Pizza, a dessert pizza that perfectly blends the succulent sweetness of cherries with the satisfying crunch of almonds. Indulge in the perfect blend of savory and sweet with our delectable pizza creation. Our mouthwatering crust is generously layered with creamy ricotta cheese, topped with succulent fresh cherries, and sprinkled with toasted almonds for a satisfying crunch. To finish it off, we add a drizzle of honey for the ultimate flavor explosion. Savor every bite of this irresistible pizza masterpiece. Indulge in the velvety goodness of creamy ricotta cheese, perfectly complemented by the burst of sweetness and vibrant red hue of cherries atop your pizza. Experience the perfect balance of flavors with our toasted almonds and sweet cherries. The delightful crunch of the almonds and the nutty flavor perfectly complement the sweetness of the cherries. Elevate your taste buds with a delicate drizzle of honey that adds a perfect touch of sweetness and enhances the overall flavor profile. Indulge your sweet tooth with the delectable Cherry Almond Pizza. This dessert pizza is the perfect combination of natural cherry sweetness and satisfying almond crunch. Savor every bite of this fantastic choice.

Makes: 1
Baking Time: 20 minutes

Ingredients:
- 1 traditional pizza dough
- ¾ cup Ground almonds
- Cherry jam
- 3 tablespoons Icing sugar, for dusting
- A few drops Almond essence
- 1½ pounds Cherries in juice (jar)
- ½ cup Flaked almonds
- ½ cup Caster sugar
- 2 egg whites
- Whipped cream, to decorate

Instructions:
a) Turn the pizza oven on at 425° F.
b) Whip the egg whites just a little bit.
c) Combine caster sugar, almond flavoring, and ground almonds in a bowl.
d) Evenly distribute the mixture over the pizza crust.
e) Top the pizza dough with flaked almonds and bake for 20 minutes.
f) In a saucepan, heat cherry jam and the saved cherry juice until they are syrupy.
g) Sprinkle icing sugar over the final pizza and top it with whipped cream and the reserved cherries.

88) *Grape & Berry Pizza*

Indulge in the delectable Grape & Berry Pizza - a tantalizing treat that pays homage to the luscious sweetness and vivid hues of grapes and berries. Savor the refreshing burst of fruity flavors in every bite. Indulge in a delectable pizza crust that's layered with rich cream cheese or mascarpone, topped with a medley of succulent grapes and berries, and finished off with a tantalizing sprinkle of sugar or a luscious drizzle of honey. Indulge in the lusciousness of our cream cheese or mascarpone, providing a velvety and creamy foundation that perfectly complements the succulent and sweet grapes and berries. Experience a delightful symphony of colors and flavors with our unique blend of assorted grapes and berries. From tangy to sweet, each bite is a harmonious balance of taste sensations. Elevate the natural sweetness of your treat with a delicate sprinkle of sugar or a luxurious drizzle of honey for an added touch of indulgence. Indulge in the delectable Grape & Berry Pizza, perfect for those who crave the refreshing and fruity essence of summer. Savor the burst of vibrant colors and flavors that will tantalize your taste buds and leave you craving for more.

Makes: 12 Servings are made.
Baking Time: 12-15 minutes

Ingredients:
- 1 Sugar Cookie Crust

CREAM CHEESE FILLING
- 1 teaspoon Vanilla extract
- 8 ounces Cream Cheese Style Spread
- 1 can Coconut milk
- ⅓ cup Powdered sugar

FRUIT TOPPING
- ¼ cup Raspberries
- 8 strawberries, sliced
- ½ cup Blueberries
- ½ cup Grapes, halved
- 4 kiwis, peeled and sliced
- 2 tablespoons Simple syrup

Instructions
a) Preheat the pizza oven to 350 degrees.
b) In a pizza pan that has been oil, spread out the cookie dough.
c) Puncture the crust with a few holes, then bake for 12 to 15 minutes. Chill.
d) Combine the cream cheese, powdered sugar, vanilla extract, and coconut milk solids in a bowl. Until smooth, blend.
e) Spread the cream cheese filling on top of the chilled cookie shell and place in the fridge.
f) Top the cold pizza with fresh berries.
g) After rubbing with simple syrup, either serve right away or chill.

89) *Fig, and Endive pizza*

Indulge in the luxurious and refined flavors of our Fig and Endive Pizza. This masterpiece harmoniously blends the luscious sweetness of figs with the tantalizingly crisp and slightly bitter taste of endive. Indulge in the ultimate pizza experience with our mouthwatering recipe. Our signature pizza crust is generously topped with tangy goat cheese or blue cheese, juicy slices of fresh figs, caramelized onions, crisp endive leaves, and a tantalizing drizzle of balsamic glaze. Savor every bite of this delectable masterpiece. Indulge in the velvety and zesty notes of goat cheese or blue cheese, perfectly complemented by the luscious sweetness of figs. Indulge in the rich and savory flavor of caramelized onions, perfectly complemented by the refreshing crunch and subtle bitterness of endive leaves. Enhance the taste with a delicate drizzle of balsamic glaze that perfectly balances the acidity and complements the overall flavor profile. Indulge in the exquisite Fig and Endive Pizza, a perfect pick for those who savor a refined and distinctive blend of flavors. This pizza boasts a delectable balance of sweet and savory notes, complemented by a tantalizing intermingling of textures and tastes.

Makes: 1 small pizza
Baking Time: 3-4 minutes

Ingredients:
- 6 oz. No-Knead Pizza Dough
- A half-cup of dry red wine
- 2 teaspoons chopped toasted walnuts
- Two ounces of cheese, chopped
- 2 teaspoons Almond oil
- 3 dried Mission figs
- Shredded half a head of Belgian endive

Instructions:
a) Combine the figs and red wine in a medium saucepan. up to a boil.
b) Switch off the heat, then leave the figs to soak. Chop them after draining.
c) Spread one tablespoon of olive oil on the pizza crust before adding the mozzarella, figs, walnuts, and shredded endive.
d) Broil the pizza for 3 to 4 minutes in the oven.
e) Just before serving, drizzle the leftover liquid over the pizza.

90) *Pizza Bianca with Peaches*

Indulge in the perfect summer treat with our Pizza Bianca with Peaches. This delectable pizza showcases the pure and refined taste of a white pizza, crowned with succulent and luscious peaches. Indulge in a mouth-watering pizza experience with our latest recipe. Our signature pizza crust is delicately brushed with premium olive oil, and seasoned with a sprinkle of sea salt and black pepper. We then add a generous layer of creamy ricotta cheese, topped with freshly sliced peaches that add a burst of natural sweetness. Finally, we finish it off with a drizzle of honey that perfectly complements the flavors. Savor every bite of this delectable pizza that is sure to leave you craving for more. Indulge in the rich and velvety taste of our olive oil base, complemented by the smooth and subtle notes of ricotta cheese. Experience the perfect balance of flavors with our sliced peaches. Each bite brings a burst of sweetness and a hint of tartness that will tantalize your taste buds. Experience a heightened level of sweetness and a delicate floral essence with just a drizzle of honey. Indulge in the delectable Pizza Bianca with Peaches - a truly exceptional choice for those seeking to relish the natural sweetness of peaches in a one-of-a-kind pizza masterpiece. Each bite captures the very essence of summer, leaving you feeling fully satisfied.

Makes: 3 servings
Baking Time: 15-20 minutes

Ingredients:
- Balsamic glaze, for drizzling
- 1 traditional Italian basic Dough
- 1 pinch Ground pepper
- 3 cloves garlic, finely chopped
- 2 peaches, sliced
- 12 ounces Mozzarella, chopped
- 2 tablespoons Olive oil
- ¼ cup Basil leaves

Instructions
a) Set the oven's temperature to 450°F.
b) Form a loose circle out of the pizza dough.
c) Olive oil should be brushed over the dough before adding chopped garlic.
d) Place the slices of peach on top.
e) Include some freshly ground pepper and the sliced mozzarella.
f) The pizza should be baked for 15 to 20 minutes.
g) Garnish with fresh basil leaves and balsamic glaze before serving.

91) *BBQ Jackfruit Pizza*

Indulge in the delectable BBQ Jackfruit Pizza, a plant-based masterpiece that highlights the remarkable adaptability of jackfruit as a meat alternative. Indulge in a mouthwatering pizza experience with our latest recipe! Savor the perfect blend of tangy and smoky barbecue sauce, paired with tender and flavorful pulled jackfruit. Topped with a variety of fresh and crisp veggies such as sliced onions, bell peppers, and vegan cheese, this pizza is sure to satisfy your cravings. Looking for a meat-free alternative to your favorite barbecue-style pizza? Look no further than jackfruit! When cooked and shredded, this versatile fruit closely mimics the texture of pulled pork or chicken, making it the perfect choice for a delicious and satisfying meal. Experience a burst of flavors and textures that will leave both vegans and non-vegans impressed. The tender jackfruit, rich barbecue sauce, and assortment of toppings come together to create a truly unforgettable taste sensation. Indulge in a guilt-free pizza experience with our BBQ Jackfruit Pizza - the perfect plant-based alternative to traditional barbecue pizza. Savor the delectable flavors and enjoy every bite!

Makes: 4 Servings
Baking Time: 13-18 minutes

Ingredients:
FOR THE PIZZA
- Two recipes for whole-wheat pizza dough
- ¼ cup of chopped red onion and ½ recipe mozzarella cheese

FOR THE JACKFRUIT
- 20 ounces of young green jackfruit from a can that has been drained and shredded.

FOR THE SAUCE
- One teaspoon of smoked paprika
- A half-cup of ketchup
- One teaspoon of garlic powder
- A quarter cup of water
- Two tablespoons of tamari and one tablespoon of maple syrup
- To taste apple cider vinegar - 1 teaspoon onion powder
- 1 teaspoon of yellow mustard

Instructions
a) Whisk all of the sauce's components together.
b) Cook the shredded jackfruit in a pan with the sauce for 8 to 10 minutes.
c) Heat the dough in the oven while the pizza oven is preheating to 425 degrees.
d) Evenly distribute the cooked jackfruit throughout the dough.
e) Top the jackfruit with a scoop of mozzarella.
f) Distribute the red onion slices across the pizza.
g) 13 to 18 minutes are needed to bake.

92) *Butternut Squash Pizza with Apples & Pecans*

Indulge in the flavors of fall with our Butternut Squash Pizza with Apples & Pecans. This delightful pizza combines the earthy notes of butternut squash, the sweet and tangy taste of apples, and the nutty crunch of pecans. Perfect for satisfying your autumn cravings. Indulge in a mouth-watering pizza experience with our latest recipe. Our signature pizza crust is generously topped with a velvety roasted butternut squash puree, delicately sliced apples, and a crunchy handful of toasted pecans. To add a touch of sophistication, we sprinkle a savory cheese blend of Gruyere or goat cheese. Savor every bite of this delectable pizza that's sure to leave you craving for more. Indulge in the velvety smoothness of roasted butternut squash puree, complemented by the crisp and juicy texture of thinly sliced apples. The perfect balance of creamy sweetness and refreshing tanginess. Experience the perfect balance of flavors and textures with our toasted pecans. The delightful crunch and rich nutty flavor will elevate your dish to the next level. Experience the perfect harmony of autumnal flavors that will take you on a journey to warm and cozy evenings by the fireplace. Indulge in the ultimate fall-inspired pizza experience with our Butternut Squash Pizza topped with crisp apples and crunchy pecans. It's the perfect choice for those who crave a comforting and seasonal meal that captures the essence of autumn.

Makes: 1 large pizza
Baking Time: about 10 minutes

Ingredients:

- One typical Italian basic dough and one-third cup of nuts, chopped.
- ½ cup of sauce made from butternut squash.
- Two tablespoons of olive oil - Two apples - Half a red onion, sliced.
- Fresh thyme leaves kosher salt, two pinches.

Instructions

a) Set the pizza oven's temperature to 450 degrees.
b) Roll out the dough onto a pizza stone or cookie sheet.
c) Employing a spoon, cover the dough with the butternut squash sauce.
d) Arrange the pecans, red onion, and apple slices on top.
e) Add kosher salt and drizzle with olive oil.
f) Bake for approximately ten minutes.
g) Add fresh thyme as a garnish, if preferred.

93) *Three-cheese and nectarine white pizza*

Indulge in the ultimate pizza experience with our Three-Cheese and Nectarine White Pizza. Savor the rich and creamy blend of three delectable cheeses, perfectly complemented by the luscious sweetness of ripe nectarines. This recipe features a pizza crust brushed with garlic-infused olive oil and topped with a mixture of ricotta cheese, mozzarella cheese, Parmesan cheese, sliced nectarines, and a sprinkle of fresh herbs such as basil or thyme. The trio of cheeses provides a rich and velvety base, while the sliced nectarines add a burst of sweetness and a delightful contrast of textures. The combination of the creamy cheeses and the juicy nectarines creates a luscious and indulgent flavor profile that will tantalize your taste buds. Three-Cheese and Nectarine White Pizza is a fantastic choice for those who appreciate the elegance of a white pizza and want to elevate it with the addition of ripe and juicy nectarines, creating a pizza that is both sophisticated and utterly delicious.

Makes: 4
Baking Time: 10-15 minutes

Ingredients:

- ½ cup grated Parmesan cheese
- Salt and freshly cracked pepper
- 1 No-Knead Pizza Dough
- 6 blackberries
- ¼ cup chopped fresh basil leaves
- 1 cup shredded mozzarella or fontina cheese
- 1 tablespoon chopped fresh chives
- 3 ounces crumbled blue cheese
- 2 tablespoons olive oil
- 1 nectarine or peach, sliced
- 1 teaspoon red pepper flakes
- Balsamic vinegar, for drizzling
- Honey, for drizzling
- 1 grated garlic clove

Instructions:

a) Heat the pizza oven to 450 degrees Fahrenheit.
b) On a surface that has been lightly sprinkled with flour, roll out the dough.
c) Place the dough on a sheet pan that has been oiled.
d) Olive oil should be brushed on the dough before chives, basil, grated garlic, and red pepper flakes are added.
e) Include blue cheese crumbles, Parmesan, and mozzarella or fontina cheese.
f) Add sliced peaches or nectarines and drizzle some extra virgin olive oil on top.
g) Add salt and pepper to taste.
h) Cook for ten to fifteen minutes.
i) Add fresh basil, blackberries, honey, balsamic vinegar, and a drizzle on the top.

94) *Sweet-Tooth Pizza*

Indulge in the delectable Sweet-Tooth Pizza, the perfect dessert option that satisfies your sweet cravings. Indulge in a decadent treat with our chocolate-hazelnut pizza recipe. A luscious layer of creamy spread is generously slathered over a crispy pizza crust, then adorned with a medley of sweet toppings. Savor the delightful combination of juicy sliced strawberries, ripe bananas, fluffy marshmallows, and a sprinkle of chocolate chips or crushed nuts. Indulge in the rich and velvety chocolate-hazelnut spread that serves as the perfect foundation for this scrumptious treat. The medley of juicy fruits and fluffy marshmallows creates a delightful explosion of sweetness and a delightful contrast of mouthfeel. Elevate your snacking experience with a delightful sprinkle of chocolate chips or crushed nuts, providing a satisfying crunch and a touch of indulgence. Indulge your sweet tooth like never before with Sweet-Tooth Pizza! Elevate your dessert game with our unique and delightful pizza experience that's guaranteed to satisfy any sweet craving.

Makes: 4 Servings
Baking Time: 20 minutes

Ingredients:

- 18 ounces refrigerated sugar cookie dough
- ½ cup halved seedless grapes
- ½ cup drained crushed pineapple
- 8 ounces whipped topping
- ½ cup sliced fresh strawberries
- ½ cup sliced banana

Instructions:

a) Bake the sugar cookie dough in the oven for 20 minutes.
b) Add whipped cream and the variety of fruits to the baked cookie batter.
c) Put the food in the fridge to chill before serving.

95) *Polynesian Pizza*

Polynesian Pizza is a tropical and vibrant pizza that combines the flavors of the Pacific Islands with a savory and satisfying pizza base. Indulge in a mouthwatering pizza experience with our signature recipe. A crispy pizza crust is smothered with a delectable blend of tangy and sweet tomato sauce, then generously topped with succulent diced ham, juicy pineapple chunks, vibrant bell peppers, and a sprinkle of shredded mozzarella cheese. Savor every bite of this irresistible combination of flavors and textures. Indulge in the perfect balance of sweet pineapple, savory ham, and tangy tomato sauce that transports your taste buds to the sunny and exotic Polynesian islands. The bell peppers add a touch of crunch and a burst of vibrant color to the pizza. Experience a slice of paradise with Polynesian Pizza! Indulge in the tropical flavors that will transport you to sandy beaches and crystal-clear waters with every bite. It's the perfect choice for those seeking a unique and delicious pizza experience.

Makes: 4 Servings
Baking Time: 16 to 18 minutes

Ingredients:
- A single recipe for authentic Italian bread dough
- 6 ounces of shredded mozzarella
- 3 ounces of diced Canadian bacon
- Half a cup of thinly cut onions
- One tablespoon of sesame seeds
- 1 cup of chunky pineapple
- Three tablespoons of soy sauce

Instructions:
a) Set the pizza oven's temperature to 450 degrees.
b) On a pizza peel or sheet pan, roll out the dough to a circle with a diameter of 14 inches.
c) Cover the dough with soy sauce and grated mozzarella.
d) Add sliced onions, pineapple chunks, and Canadian bacon to the pizza's toppings.
e) Sprinkle sesame seeds over the top.
f) For 16 to 18 minutes, cook or grill.

96) *Pesto and Dried Cranberry Pizza*

Experience a burst of flavor with our Pesto and Dried Cranberry Pizza. This one-of-a-kind combination brings together the vibrant and aromatic flavors of pesto with the tart and slightly sweet taste of dried cranberries. Indulge in a mouthwatering pizza experience with our signature recipe. Our crispy pizza crust is adorned with a luscious spread of either homemade or store-bought pesto sauce. A generous sprinkle of shredded mozzarella cheese adds a creamy texture, while plump dried cranberries provide a burst of tangy sweetness. Savor every bite of this delectable creation! Indulge in the exquisite taste of our pesto sauce, crafted from a harmonious blend of fresh basil, garlic, pine nuts, Parmesan cheese, and olive oil. Savor the burst of herbal and garlicky goodness in every bite. Experience the perfect balance of chewy texture and tangy flavor with our dried cranberries, expertly paired with our delicious pesto. Indulge in a one-of-a-kind pizza experience that tantalizes your taste buds with a perfect balance of savory and sweet flavors. Indulge in the delectable Pesto and Dried Cranberry Pizza - a tantalizing take on the classic pizza that promises to tantalize your taste buds with its unique blend of flavors. Savor every bite and experience a burst of flavors that will leave you craving for more.

Makes: 1 pizza
Baking Time: 16 to 18 minutes

Ingredients:
- One traditional Italian basic dough recipe
- 1½ ounces of shredded Fontina
- 6 table spoons of chopped dried cranberries
- 6 table spoons of pizza pesto

Instructions:
a) Holding the edges, carefully rotate and stretch the dough into a circle with a 14-inch diameter.
b) Evenly cover the crust with the pesto.
c) Cover the pesto with the shredded Fontina.
d) Top the cheese with the chopped dry cranberries.
e) Cook the pizza on the grill or in the oven for 16 to 18 minutes, or until the cheese is melted and the dough is brown.

97) *Mango Pizza with Black Beans*

Indulge in a tropical and satisfying pizza experience with our Mango Pizza featuring the juicy sweetness of mangoes and the earthy flavor and creamy texture of black beans. Indulge in a mouth-watering pizza experience with our latest recipe. Our signature pizza crust is smothered with a tangy tomato sauce, topped with a generous amount of black beans, diced ripe mangoes, thinly sliced red onions, and a sprinkle of shredded cheddar or Mexican cheese blend. Savor every bite of this delectable treat! Indulge in the luscious sweetness of ripe mangoes that perfectly complement the hearty and savory black beans. Indulge in the perfect pizza experience with a harmonious blend of flavors that will leave your taste buds fully satisfied. This deliciously refreshing and filling pizza is a must-try! Experience a burst of flavor with our thinly sliced red onions that add just the right amount of sharpness. And with our shredded cheese, you'll enjoy a creamy and melty finish that will leave your taste buds wanting more. Indulge in the exotic and flavorful Mango Pizza with Black Beans, the perfect addition to your pizza collection. This unique fusion of tropical ingredients will whisk you away to a paradise of sun, sand, and palm trees with every delectable bite.

Makes: 6 servings
Baking Time: about 15 minutes

Ingredients:
- 1 traditional pizza crust made in Italy
- ¼ cup washed and cooked black beans
- 1 chopped green onion
- ¾ cup of shredded Mexican cheese
- ½ cup of sliced Zucchini
- ½ cup of sliced Mango
- ¾ cup of spicy salsa
- One-quarter cup of cilantro leaves

Instructions
a) Place the pizza dough on a sheet pan, then top it with the hot salsa.
b) Top the salsa with the crumbled Mexican cheese.
c) Add black beans, zucchini, and mango slices on top.
d) Bake the pizza at the recommended temperature for the crust for 15 minutes or until the cheese is melted and bubbling.
e) Before serving, garnish with chopped green onions and cilantro leaves.

98) *Strawberry Pizza with Mild Microgreens*

Indulge in the delectable and visually stunning Strawberry Pizza with Mild Microgreens. This pizza perfectly blends the sweetness of fresh strawberries with the delicate and subtle flavors of mild microgreens. Indulge in a mouth-watering pizza crust that's generously layered with creamy and tangy cheese - think goat cheese or cream cheese - and topped with fresh, juicy strawberries. Sprinkled with mild microgreens and finished off with a tantalizing drizzle of balsamic glaze, this recipe is a true feast for the senses. Indulge in the luxurious creaminess of the cheese base, perfectly complemented by the tangy sweetness of the vibrant strawberries. Experience the freshness of mild microgreens like baby spinach or arugula, perfectly paired with the delightful touch of acidity from our balsamic glaze. Elevate your pizza game and enhance the overall flavor profile with this winning combination. Indulge in the exquisite Strawberry Pizza with Mild Microgreens - a pizza that's not only visually stunning but also a perfect blend of sweet and savory flavors. This pizza is a refreshing and sophisticated treat that celebrates the essence of the season.

Makes: 1
Baking Time: 20 minutes

Ingredients:
- 1 table scoop of pizza sauce - 1 basic Italian traditional dough
- A small amount of mildly mixed microgreens
- Strawberries, ½ cup
- ¼ cup cheese

Instructions:
a) Form a 10-inch-diameter disc out of the dough by rolling it out on a surface dusted with flour.
b) Cover the dough with the pizza sauce equally.
c) Put the dough in the oven with the pizza and bake it there until the cheese is melted and the crust is brown.
d) Arrange some mild microgreens, shredded cheese, and strawberry slices on top of the pizza.
e) Present and enjoy.

CHAPTER 7: VEGAN PIZZA

99) *Shiitake Tofu Pizza*

Pizza with shiitake mushrooms and tofu is a delectable and healthy option for vegetarians and vegans. A tasty tomato sauce, sautéed shiitake mushrooms, marinated tofu cubes, vegan cheese, and a variety of fresh herbs are added to a pizza dough in this recipe. The marinated tofu adds a pleasing texture and a source of plant-based protein, and the shiitake mushrooms give a rich and delicious umami taste. These ingredients work together to produce a tasty, filling, and wholesome pizza that is hearty and fulfilling. For those wishing to experiment with novel and intriguing flavors in their plant-based pizza concoctions, shiitake tofu pizza is a fantastic option.

Makes: 1 Large Pizza
Baking Time: 16 to 18 minutes

Ingredients:
- 1 recipe for traditional Italian basic dough
- 1 teaspoon soy sauce
- 8 ounces soft silken tofu
- 6 ounces sliced shiitake mushrooms
- 3 ounces sliced medium scallions
- 2 teaspoons Asian red chili pastes
- 1 teaspoon toasted sesame oil

Instructions:
a) Roll out the dough into a circle that is 14 inches in diameter on a pizza peel or sheet pan by carefully turning and extending it while holding the edges.
b) To make the tofu creamy, blend it in a food processor.
c) Evenly cover the crust with the creamy tofu.
d) Scatter sliced shiitake mushrooms and scallions on top of the tofu.
e) To the toppings, add equal parts soy sauce, ginger, chili paste, and toasted sesame oil.
f) Cook or grill the pizza for 16 to 18 minutes, or until the toppings are heated through and the crust is brown.

100) *Vegan Margherita Pizza*

Vegan Margherita Pizza is a traditional Italian pizza with a plant-based twist that may be consumed by people on a vegan diet. The pizza dough in this recipe is covered with a zesty tomato sauce, fresh tomato slices, dairy-free mozzarella cheese, and fresh basil leaves. The freshness of the tomatoes are complemented by the tangy tomato sauce's explosion of flavor, and the dairy-free mozzarella cheese gives the pizza a creamy, melty texture. The basil leaves enhance the flavor of the pizza by adding a hint of herbal perfume. For individuals who follow a vegan lifestyle and want to enjoy a familiar and comforting pizza experience, vegan margherita pizza is an excellent option. It demonstrates the adaptability of plant-based ingredients and demonstrates that vegan pizzas can be just as tasty and enjoyable as their non-vegan counterparts.

Makes: 1 Large Pizza
Baking Time: about 12 minutes

Ingredients:
- 1 Traditional Italian basic Dough
- ¼ cup Basil pesto
- 1 tablespoon Nutritional yeast
- 2 plum tomatoes, thinly sliced
- 1½ tablespoons Olive oil
- 1 cup Firm tofu, drained
- Salt and cracked black pepper

Instructions:
a) Carefully transfer the dough to a sheet pan or other pan that has been greased.
b) Mix the drained tofu, salt, pepper, and nutritional yeast thoroughly in a food processor.
c) Apply the olive oil to the prepared pizza dough in an even layer using your fingertips.
d) Evenly distribute the tofu mixture over the dough.
e) Spread the basil pesto over the tofu mixture after combining it with the remaining olive oil.
f) Spread salt and pepper on top of the pizza before adding the tomato pieces.
g) Bake the pizza at 450 degrees Fahrenheit for about 12 minutes, or until the crust is crisp and golden.

101) *Tofu and Capers Pizza*

Indulge in a one-of-a-kind culinary experience with our Tofu and Capers Pizza. This delectable pizza boasts a creamy tofu base perfectly complemented by the briny and tangy notes of capers. Savor every bite of this unique and flavorful creation. Indulge in a delectable pizza experience with our signature recipe. Our crust is perfectly complemented by a luscious layer of creamy tofu spread, topped with a sprinkle of capers and sliced red onions. To add the perfect finishing touch, we drizzle a generous amount of extra-virgin olive oil. Indulge in the velvety smoothness of our creamy tofu spread, perfectly complemented by the zesty bursts of briny capers. Elevate your pizza experience with this tantalizing combination of textures and flavors. Experience the perfect balance of sharpness and sweetness with our expertly sliced red onions. Discover the endless possibilities of tofu with our delectable Tofu and Capers Pizza. Elevate your pizza game with this unique blend of flavors that will tantalize your taste buds. Indulge in a delectable and fulfilling choice that accommodates both vegetarian and vegan lifestyles. Experience an explosion of savory and tangy tastes that will leave your taste buds yearning for more.

Makes: 1 Large Pizza
Baking Time: 10 minutes

Ingredients:
- 3 garlic cloves, chopped
- ¼ cup sliced sun-dried tomatoes
- 2 tablespoons fresh parsley, chopped
- 1 teaspoon dried oregano
- 16 ounces tofu, drained and sliced
- Pinch of salt
- 14½ ounces canned diced tomatoes, drained
- 1 tablespoon capers
- 2 tablespoons olive oil
- ½ teaspoon sugar
- Cracked black pepper

Instructions
a) Set the oven's temperature to 275°F.
b) Golden-brown the tofu slices in an oiled skillet. Add salt and pepper to taste.
c) Fry the minced garlic for a minute in the hotter residual oil.
d) Include the sun-dried tomatoes, capers, oregano, sugar, salt, and chopped tomatoes that have been drained. roughly 10 minutes of cooking.
e) Cover the fried tofu pieces with the prepared sauce and sprinkle chopped parsley on top.

102) *BBQ Tofu Pizza with Pepper Jack*

Indulge in the mouthwatering BBQ Tofu Pizza with Pepper Jack! This delectable pizza is a perfect blend of smoky and tangy BBQ sauce, creamy tofu, and spicy pepper jack cheese. Satisfy your cravings with every bite of this flavorful pizza. Indulge in a mouthwatering pizza experience with our delectable recipe. Our signature pizza crust is generously layered with tangy BBQ sauce, topped with sliced and marinated tofu, and sprinkled with shredded pepper jack cheese. To add a pop of color and flavor, we've added a selection of vibrant vegetables such as bell peppers and red onions. Savor every bite of this irresistible pizza creation. Indulge in the delectable combination of savory tofu and melty pepper jack cheese, perfectly complemented by the rich and smoky flavor of our BBQ sauce. Indulge in a truly satisfying pizza experience with our bold combination of flavors. Packed with deliciousness, every bite is hearty and fulfilling. Indulge in the mouthwatering BBQ Tofu Pizza with Pepper Jack! This delectable pizza is a perfect pick for those who crave a protein-packed and flavorful meal. The pizza showcases the versatility of tofu and adds a spicy twist to the classic BBQ pizza.

Makes: 2
Baking Time: 12-14 minutes

Ingredients:
- 2 recipes No Rise Spelt Crust

SRIRACHA BBQ TOFU
- 1 cup pressed and cubed tofu
- 2 tablespoons BBQ sauce
- 3 teaspoons Sriracha
- ½ teaspoon garlic powder

OTHER TOPPINGS:
- Sliced red bell peppers
- Pasta/marinara sauce
- Sliced onions
- Almond Milk Pepper Jack

Instructions
a) Set the pizza oven's temperature to 450° F.
b) Combine the BBQ sauce, Sriracha, and garlic powder in a bowl. Toss in the cubes of pressed tofu after adding them.
c) Spread marinara sauce over the pizza dough.
d) Arrange the red bell pepper slices, onions, and any additional vegetables you want on top.
e) Add salt and pepper to taste.
f) Place the marinated tofu pieces on top and drizzle with any leftover Sriracha BBQ sauce.
g) Add as much Almond Milk Pepper Jack cheese as you like on top.
h) Put the pizzas in the oven for 12 to 14 minutes.
i) Add chopped cilantro as a garnish before slicing and serving.

103) *Portobello and Black Olive Pizza*

Indulge in the delectable Portobello and Black Olive Pizza, boasting a rich and savory blend of meaty portobello mushrooms and briny black olives. Satisfy your cravings with this earthy and slightly bitter flavor combination. Indulge in the perfect pizza experience with our mouth-watering recipe. Featuring a crispy crust, generously layered with tangy tomato sauce, grilled or sautéed portobello mushroom slices, sliced black olives, and a sprinkle of grated Parmesan cheese. Savor every bite of this delectable treat! Indulge in the rich and satisfying texture of portobello mushrooms that will remind you of a meaty bite. Complemented by the bold and distinctive flavor of black olives, this pizza is a true taste sensation. Experience a delectable and savory finish with our grated Parmesan cheese, perfectly seasoned with a touch of saltiness. Indulge in the savory and delectable Portobello and Black Olive Pizza - a true delight for those who relish the bold flavors of mushrooms and olives. This pizza is a celebration of the richness and depth of these ingredients, providing a truly satisfying culinary experience.

Makes: 1 Large Pizza
Baking Time: about 12 minutes

Ingredients:
- 1 Traditional Italian basic Dough
- ½ cup pizza sauce or marinara sauce
- 2 portobello mushroom caps, sliced
- 1 tablespoon fresh basil, chopped
- ¼ teaspoon dried oregano
- 2 tablespoons olive oil
- Salt and cracked black pepper

Instructions:
a) Holding the edges, carefully rotate and stretch the dough into a circle with a 14-inch diameter.
b) Cook the sliced portobello mushroom caps in one tablespoon of olive oil in a skillet over medium heat for five minutes.
c) Season the mushrooms with salt and freshly cracked black pepper and add the chopped basil and dried oregano.
d) Mix the mushrooms with the black olive slices, then leave the mixture aside.
e) Then, evenly distribute the remaining tablespoon of olive oil over the prepared pizza dough.
f) Cover the dough with the marinara or pizza sauce.
g) Evenly distribute the veggie mixture over the sauce.
h) Bake the pizza for 12 minutes at 450°F, or until the toppings are heated through and the crust is brown.

104) *White Mushroom Pizza*

Indulge in the exquisite White Mushroom Pizza, crafted to highlight the subtle and earthy notes of premium mushrooms. This pizza is a true delight for your taste buds and a feast for your eyes. Indulge in a delectable pizza experience with our signature recipe. Our pizza crust is perfectly complemented by a luscious white sauce, infused with either béchamel or garlic cream. The sautéed white mushrooms add a delightful texture, while the grated Gruyère or Fontina cheese provides a burst of flavor. To top it off, we've added a selection of fresh herbs to elevate the taste to a whole new level. Indulge in the luxurious and smooth foundation of our white sauce, perfectly complementing the delectable taste of our savory mushrooms. Indulge in the savory and satisfying sautéed white mushrooms that boast a tender and meaty texture. Complemented by the nutty and melty grated cheese, this dish is sure to tantalize your taste buds. Experience a burst of freshness and brightness with the addition of our hand-picked, premium quality fresh herbs. Indulge in the exquisite taste of White Mushroom Pizza, perfect for those who appreciate a refined and sophisticated pizza experience. This pizza is expertly crafted to highlight the earthy and subtle flavors of mushrooms, making it a fantastic choice for any discerning palate.

Makes: 1 Large Pizza
Baking Time: about 12 minutes

Ingredients:
- 1 cup sliced white mushrooms
- Sun-dried tomatoes
- 1 Traditional Italian basic Dough
- ½ cup sliced red onion
- Sauteed zucchini
- Salt and cracked black pepper
- ¼ cup chopped red bell pepper
- Sliced hot peppers
- 2 tablespoons olive oil
- 2 tablespoons sliced Kalamata olives
- ½ cup pizza sauce or marinara sauce
- ¼ teaspoon dried basil
- Artichoke hearts

Instructions:
a) Holding the edges, carefully rotate and stretch the dough into a circle with a 14-inch diameter.
b) In a skillet, cook the red bell pepper, white mushrooms, and red onion in hot olive oil until tender.
c) Add the final tablespoon of olive oil to the pizza dough that is prepared for baking.
d) Cover the dough with the marinara or pizza sauce and sprinkle with dried basil.
e) Spoon the sautéed veggie mixture evenly over the sauce.
f) Add salt and freshly ground black pepper to taste.
g) Include any other garnishes you'd like, along with the sliced Kalamata olives.
h) Bake the pizza for 12 minutes at 450°F or until the crust is crisp and golden.

105) *Red Lentil Pizza Crust*

Indulge in a guilt-free pizza experience with our Red Lentil Pizza Crust - a gluten-free and protein-packed alternative to the conventional pizza crusts. Indulge in a delectable pizza crust that boasts a unique blend of red lentils, water, and a carefully curated selection of herbs and spices. Indulge in the rich and velvety texture of our red lentil batter, carefully crafted by soaking and blending the finest lentils. Once spread onto a baking sheet, our batter is baked to perfection, resulting in a delectable golden crispiness that will leave your taste buds wanting more. Experience a crust like no other - one that is not only free from gluten, but also packed with fiber and essential nutrients. Indulge in the ultimate pizza experience with our Red Lentil Pizza Crust. Its versatility allows you to personalize your pizza with your favorite toppings, making every bite a unique and satisfying one. Indulge in your pizza cravings with our versatile crust that serves as the perfect base for your culinary masterpieces. Whether you're a fan of the classic tomato sauce and cheese or crave a medley of fresh veggies and plant-based proteins, our crust offers a wholesome and delectable canvas for your pizza creations. Indulge in a healthy and flavorful pizza experience with our Red Lentil Pizza Crust - the perfect choice for those with dietary restrictions or anyone seeking a delicious twist on traditional pizza.

Makes: 1 Large Pizza
Baking Time: 13-18 minutes

Ingredients:
- ¾ cup water
- ¾ cup dry split red lentils, uncooked
- ¾ teaspoon sea salt
- 1 pinch of basil
- 1 pinch of oregano
- 1 pinch of garlic powder
- Optional: Vegan Toppings

Instructions
a) Puree the red lentils, water, sea salt, basil, oregano, and garlic powder in a blender or food processor until smooth.
b) Spoon the lentil mixture thinly and evenly onto a circle on a pizza tray coated with parchment paper.
c) After 16 minutes of baking at 400 degrees Fahrenheit, carefully turn the crust over.
d) Add the toppings of your choice, such as vegan cheeses, vegetables, or pizza sauce.
e) Bake the pizza for a further 3 to 5 minutes, or until the crust is crispy and the toppings are well heated.

106) *Spicy Pinto Bean Pizza*

Indulge in the bold and flavorful Spicy Pinto Bean Pizza, crafted to perfection with protein-rich pinto beans. This hearty and nutritious meal is sure to satisfy your cravings. Indulge in a mouth-watering pizza experience with our signature recipe. Our crispy pizza crust is generously topped with a zesty tomato sauce, followed by a layer of perfectly seasoned and mashed pinto beans. A sprinkle of spicy jalapeno peppers adds a kick of flavor, while a selection of your favorite toppings such as diced tomatoes, red onions, and cilantro complete this culinary masterpiece. Savor every bite of this delicious pizza that will leave you craving for more. Indulge in the creamy and nutty texture of the pinto beans, perfectly complemented by the fiery kick of jalapeno peppers. This pizza is sure to elevate your taste buds with its irresistible spiciness. Indulge in a one-of-a-kind pizza experience that tantalizes your taste buds with a perfect blend of flavors. Satisfy your cravings with every bite of this delicious pizza that packs a punch of heat. Discover a world of bold and exciting flavors with our Spicy Pinto Bean Pizza. Perfect for those seeking to add more plant-based proteins to their pizza repertoire, this delicious option is sure to satisfy your cravings and tantalize your taste buds.

Makes: 1
Baking Time: about 12 minutes

Ingredients:
- 1 Traditional Italian basic Dough
- 2 tablespoons chopped cilantro
- 1 tablespoon olive oil
- 2 tablespoons chopped green chiles
- 1 ½ cups cooked pinto beans, drained
- 1 cup tomato salsa
- 2 tablespoons sliced Kalamata olives
- 1 teaspoon chili powder

Instructions:
a) Set the oven's temperature to what the pizza dough requires.
b) Place the dough onto a sheet pan or pizza pan that has been greased.
c) Add cooked pinto beans to hot olive oil in a skillet. Add chili powder, then simmer for about five minutes.
d) Take the beans from the heat and thoroughly mash them. To add moisture, spread the salsa over the mashed beans.
e) Evenly cover the prepared pizza dough with the bean mixture.
f) Drizzle any leftover salsa over the bean mixture and top with sliced olives and chopped green chilies.
g) Bake the pizza for approximately 12 minutes, or until the crust is crisp and golden.
h) Before serving, garnish with chopped cilantro.

107) *BBQ Corn Jalapeno Sweet Potato Pizza*

Indulge in the delectable BBQ Corn Jalapeno Sweet Potato Pizza, a tantalizing blend of flavors that marries the rich sweetness of roasted sweet potatoes, the bold smokiness of BBQ sauce, the fiery kick of jalapeno peppers, and the delightful sweetness of corn kernels. Indulge in the ultimate pizza experience with our mouth-watering recipe! Our signature pizza crust is generously topped with a delectable blend of tangy and smoky BBQ sauce, perfectly roasted sweet potato slices, a tantalizing scattering of spicy jalapeno peppers, a delightful sprinkle of golden corn kernels, and a finishing drizzle of premium olive oil. Savor every bite of this irresistible masterpiece! Indulge in the mouth-watering combination of creamy and slightly caramelized roasted sweet potatoes, perfectly balanced with tangy BBQ sauce. The spicy kick of jalapeno peppers adds an extra layer of depth to this delectable pizza. Experience the perfect balance of flavors with the addition of sweet bursts from the corn kernels. Indulge in the perfect blend of sweet, smoky, and spicy with our BBQ Corn Jalapeno Sweet Potato Pizza. It's the ultimate choice for those who crave a flavor explosion in every bite. Experience a pizza like no other with a unique twist that highlights the versatility of ingredients such as sweet potatoes and jalapenos.

Makes: 1
Baking Time: 16 to 18 minutes

Ingredients:
- 1 Traditional Italian Pizza Crust
- 1 sliced jalapeno
- ½ onion, sliced thick
- 1 sweet potato, cubed and boiled
- Peppers or other veggies
- ⅓ cup BBQ sauce
- ⅓ cup cooked corn kernels
- 3 teaspoons BBQ seasoning

Instructions
a) Combine sweet potatoes that have been boiled, corn kernels that have been cooked, sliced onions, peppers, or other vegetables, 2 table spoons of BBQ sauce, and a dash of black pepper in a bowl.
b) Use the pizza dough to make a thin-crust pizza.
c) Apply olive oil to the pizza dough.
d) Evenly cover the pizza dough with the sweet potato mixture and jalapeno slices.
e) Season the vegetables with barbecue seasoning.
f) Top with the leftover BBQ sauce.
g) Bake the pizza for 16 to 18 minutes at 425°F, or until the toppings are heated through and the crust is brown.
h) Cut and present.

108) *Creamed Corn Pizza*

Indulge in the velvety goodness of Creamed Corn Pizza, a delectable pie that boasts the luscious and comforting taste of creamed corn. Indulge in a mouth-watering pizza experience with our latest recipe. Our signature pizza crust is smothered with a luscious layer of creamy corn sauce, topped with a generous sprinkle of grated cheese, and adorned with a selection of your favorite toppings. Savor the crispy bacon, diced bell peppers, and fresh herbs that come together to create a symphony of flavors. Indulge in the luxurious creamed corn sauce that forms the velvety and slightly sweet base of this pizza. Topped with grated cheese, it adds a savory and melty element that will leave your taste buds craving for more. Elevate your pizza game with our delectable toppings that offer a tantalizing blend of textures and flavors, resulting in a truly indulgent and satisfying pizza experience. Indulge in the ultimate comfort food with our Creamed Corn Pizza. This one-of-a-kind pizza boasts a delightful blend of sweet and creamy flavors that will tantalize your taste buds. Indulge in a delectable choice that evokes a sense of fond memories and coziness to your pizza evening.

Makes: 3 servings
Baking Time: about 15-17 minutes

Ingredients:
- ½ recipe of Traditional Italian basic Dough
- 10 grape or cherry tomatoes, halved
- ½ onion, chopped
- Black pepper and red pepper flakes (optional)
- ½ cup Chorizo crumbles
- 6 fresh basil leaves
FOR THE CREAMED CORN SAUCE
- ½ cup canned coconut milk
- 1 tablespoon nutritional yeast
- 1¾ cups thawed corn kernels, divided
- ¾ teaspoon sea salt
- 2 tablespoons softened butter
- 2 tablespoons tapioca starch
- 1 clove garlic
- 1 teaspoon cane sugar

Instructions
a) Blend 1¾ cups of corn kernels and the rest ingredients for the creamed corn sauce in a blender until completely smooth.
b) The pizza dough should be rolled out into a 12-inch round.
c) Lay the dough out on a pizza stone or sheet pan.
d) Cover the dough with roughly half of the creamed corn sauce.
e) Add the remaining ½ cup of corn kernels on top, along with the chopped onion, halved tomatoes, and Chorizo crumbles.
f) Baking the pizza for 15–17 minutes, or until the toppings are cooked and the crust is golden.
g) Add fresh basil leaves as a garnish and, if preferred, some black pepper and red pepper flakes.
h) Cut and present.

109) *Zucchini Pepperoni Pizza*

Indulge in a healthier and more imaginative version of the classic pepperoni pizza with our Zucchini Pepperoni Pizza. Our recipe replaces the conventional cured meat with delectable and nourishing zucchini slices, adding a burst of flavor to every bite. Indulge in a mouth-watering pizza experience with our signature recipe. A crispy pizza crust is smothered with a tangy tomato sauce, layered with thinly sliced zucchini, and topped off with a generous sprinkle of grated cheese. Customize your pizza with your favorite toppings, from savory black olives to fragrant fresh basil and spicy red pepper flakes. Savor every bite of this delectable creation! Indulge in the perfect blend of textures with our zucchini pizza. The tender and slightly crunchy zucchini slices are perfectly complemented by the tangy tomato sauce and grated cheese, bringing you the familiar flavors of a traditional pizza. Experience an explosion of flavor and freshness with our delectable additional toppings. Indulge in the delectable Zucchini Pepperoni Pizza, a perfect pick for those seeking to add more veggies to their pizza or for those who crave a vegetarian or lighter option to the traditional pepperoni pizza. Indulge in a delectable and fulfilling choice that lets you relish the taste of a classic pizza with a wholesome spin.

Makes: 2
Baking Time: 12-15 minutes

Ingredients:
- 2 tablespoons tomato paste
- 1 recipe for Traditional Italian basic Dough
- 2 zucchini, sliced
- 2 tablespoons balsamic vinegar
- 6 ounces vegan Mozzarella cheese
- Hot sauce

Instructions
a) Set the oven for pizza at 390°F.
b) Combine spicy sauce, tamari, and balsamic vinegar in a baking dish.
c) Include the zucchini slices and completely cover them in the marinade.
d) Refrigerate the dish for the night.
e) Evenly smear tomato paste on the pizza crust. Slices of marinated zucchini should be arranged on top.
f) Top the pizza with vegan Mozzarella cheese.
g) Bake the pizza in the oven for about 15 minutes, or until the cheese has melted and the crust is brown.
h) Cut and present.

110) *Vegan Caprese Pizza*

Indulge in the refreshing and delightful Vegan Caprese Pizza, a modern take on the classic Italian Caprese salad. This plant-based and dairy-free twist is sure to tantalize your taste buds. Indulge in the ultimate pizza experience with our mouth-watering recipe. A crispy pizza crust is generously layered with tangy tomato sauce, topped with juicy slices of fresh tomato, and smothered with dairy-free mozzarella cheese. To add a touch of freshness, we sprinkle a handful of fragrant basil leaves on top. Savor every bite of this delicious masterpiece! Indulge in the delectable blend of juicy tomatoes, velvety vegan cheese, and aromatic basil, evoking the classic Caprese salad. Indulge in the luscious creaminess of our vegan mozzarella cheese, which perfectly mimics the rich texture of dairy-based cheese. Indulge in the delectable Vegan Caprese Pizza, perfect for those who follow a dairy-free or vegan diet. Savor the invigorating and lively flavors of a Caprese salad in every bite. Experience the delight of simplicity with our light and satisfying option that highlights the versatility of plant-based alternatives to traditional dairy products. Discover the beauty of simple ingredients in every bite.

Makes: 3 Servings
Baking Time: 21 minutes

Ingredients:

- 1 pound multigrain pizza dough
- Red pepper flakes (if desired)
- 1 tablespoon nutritional yeast
- ⅔ cup filtered water
- 3 cloves garlic, chopped
- Sliced fresh basil leaves
- 1 teaspoon salt
- ½ cup raw cashews
- 1 tablespoon arrowroot powder
- 1 tablespoon apple cider vinegar
- 2 tablespoons olive oil
- 3 ripe Roma tomatoes, sliced
- Balsamic Reduction

Instructions

a) Turn on the oven to 400°F.
b) On a baking sheet, roll out the pizza dough into a 15-inch circle.
c) The crust should be faintly brown after 7 minutes in the oven.
d) Blend filtered water, raw cashews, nutritional yeast, arrowroot, apple cider vinegar, and salt in a food processor. Until smooth, blend.
e) Place the mixture in a pot, then heat it for 5 minutes while stirring constantly.
f) Drizzle olive oil over the baked crust and top with minced garlic.
g) Evenly distribute the cashew mixture over the crust.
h) Spoon the thinly sliced tomatoes over the sauce.
i) Bake the pizza for a further 8 to 14 minutes, or until the toppings are heated through and the crust is crispy.
j) Add sliced fresh basil leaves and drizzle with balsamic reduction.
k) Enjoy

CHAPTER 8: GLUTEN-FREE PIZZA

111) *Gluten-Free Salad Pizza*

Indulge in the refreshing and nutritious Gluten-Free Salad Pizza, a delightful twist on the classic pizza that's perfect for those who follow a gluten-free lifestyle. Indulge in a mouth-watering pizza experience with our gluten-free crust recipe, complemented by a colorful array of crisp and fresh salad toppings. Indulge in a burst of freshness with our signature toppings, featuring a vibrant array of crisp vegetables including lettuce, juicy tomatoes, crunchy cucumbers, and zesty bell peppers. Elevate your taste buds with the savory addition of olives, feta cheese, and a tantalizing drizzle of tangy vinaigrette or pesto. Indulge in a pizza that's not only light and refreshing but also packed with wholesome ingredients. Indulge in the delectable flavors of a well-crafted salad with our Gluten-Free Salad Pizza. It's the perfect option for those seeking a lighter alternative to traditional pizza without compromising on taste.

Makes: 1 pizza
Baking Time: 20 minutes

Ingredients:
- Pizza Dough Without Gluten
- 1 tablespoon mayonnaise
- ¼ cup olive oil
- 1 coarsely grated garlic clove;
- ½ tea spoon Italian seasoning
- Salt and freshly ground black pepper
- 3 cups of your favorite salad greens
- ½ cup of finely chopped Parmesan cheese
- 1 cup of onion slices
- ⅓ cup of sliced pickled pepperoncini
- 3 table spoons red wine vinegar

Instructions:
a) Spread the gluten-free pizza dough out on a sheet pan that has been lined or greased.
b) To mold the dough into a circular, thinner shape, use your fingers.
c) Sprinkle flaky salt and pepper on top of the dough surface and drizzle a little olive oil over it.
d) Bake the pizza dough at 400 degrees for about 20 minutes.
e) Combine mayonnaise, grated garlic, olive oil, vinegar, Italian seasoning, salt, and pepper in a mixing bowl.
f) Top the baked pizza crust with salad greens, thinly sliced onion, Parmesan cheese, and pickled pepperoncini slices right before serving.
g) Slice the pizza and serve it.

112) _Gluten-Free Margherita Pizza_

Indulge in the timeless and classic taste of Margherita Pizza, now available in a gluten-free crust option. Indulge in a mouth-watering gluten-free pizza crust that's topped with a delectable combination of fresh tomatoes, creamy mozzarella cheese, and fragrant basil leaves. Enhance the flavors of your toppings with a delicate drizzle of premium olive oil and a light sprinkle of salt and pepper. Indulge in a pizza that boasts a delightful balance of lightness and cheesiness, while allowing the natural flavors of the ingredients to shine through. Indulge in the classic flavors of Margherita pizza without any gluten worries. Our Gluten-Free Margherita Pizza is the perfect choice for those with dietary restrictions or gluten sensitivities. Savor every bite without sacrificing taste or texture.

Makes: 1 Large Pizza
Baking Time: 30-35 minutes

Ingredients:
- 1 gluten-free dough recipe
- One tablespoon of olive oil
- 1 cup of tomato slices
- ½ cup of shredded mozzarella cheese
- One and a half tablespoons of grated Parmesan cheese
- Pepper and salt
- Quartered cherry tomatoes, equaling ½ cup
- fresh basil

Instructions:
a) Distribute the tomato slices across the gluten-free dough.
b) Sprinkle the pizza with the shredded Mozzarella cheese.
c) Top with grated Parmesan cheese.
d) Add salt and pepper to the pizza and drizzle some olive oil over it.
e) For 30-35 minutes, bake the pizza.
f) Tear fresh basil leaves and put them over the finished pizza.
g) Cut and plate.

113) _Gluten-Free Detroit-Style Pizza_

Indulge in the mouth-watering Gluten-Free Detroit-Style Pizza, a delectable variation that caters to your gluten-free lifestyle. Indulge in a delectable pizza experience with our gluten-free crust that boasts a one-of-a-kind thick and square shape. Experience the perfect pizza crust with our expertly crafted baking technique. Our well-oiled pan ensures a crispy and golden exterior, while the interior remains soft and fluffy. Indulge in a mouthwatering pizza experience with our generous amount of melted cheese, tangy tomato sauce, and a variety of toppings such as savory pepperoni, flavorful onions, and crisp bell peppers. Indulge in a pizza that is packed with flavor, heartiness, and satisfaction. Our gluten-free crust is the perfect base for the robust toppings, creating a delightful combination of textures that will leave your taste buds wanting more. Indulge in the delectable Gluten-Free Detroit-Style Pizza, a perfect choice for those seeking a gluten-free option that doesn't compromise on flavor and consistency. Experience the authentic essence of this beloved pizza style with every bite.

Makes: 2
Baking Time: about 25 minutes

Ingredients:
- 2 recipes of gluten-free dough
- ⅓ cup sliced pepperoni
- 2 cups shredded Mozzarella cheese
- Dried oregano
- Honey for drizzling
- ¾ cup marinara sauce
- Chili flakes

Instructions:
a) Cover the borders of an oiled pan with the gluten-free dough.
b) Cover the dough with the shredded mozzarella cheese by spreading it from the middle of the pan outward.
c) Place pieces of pepperoni and marinara sauce on top.
d) Bake the pizza at 500 degrees for about 25 minutes on the bottom rack.
e) To remove the pizza from the pan, use a knife.
f) As garnishes, add honey, chile flakes, and dried oregano.
g) Cut and plate.

114) *Gluten-Free Deep Dish Pizza*

Indulge in the savory and satisfying Gluten-Free Deep Dish Pizza, the perfect choice for those who prefer a gluten-free diet. Indulge in a mouth-watering pizza experience with our gluten-free deep dish crust. Its sturdy and dense texture is the perfect foundation for a generous amount of toppings and sauce. Indulge in a delectable pie with a crust crafted from a blend of premium gluten-free flours. Our crust is pre-baked to perfection, ensuring a crispy texture that perfectly complements the flavorful combination of ingredients within. Indulge in a plethora of topping options for your pizza, including savory Italian sausage, flavorful peppers and onions, and a luscious tomato sauce. Indulge in a mouth-watering pizza that boasts a crispy, golden crust. Each bite is packed with satisfying flavors that will leave you feeling content. Indulge in the ultimate pizza experience with our Gluten-Free Deep Dish Pizza. Savor every bite of this delectable alternative that boasts the same great taste and texture as traditional pizza. Don't compromise on flavor - choose our gluten-free option and enjoy a satisfying and guilt-free meal.

Makes: 1 pizza
Baking Time: 20-25 minutes

Ingredients:
- 1 recipe Gluten-Free Pizza Dough
- ¾ cup pizza sauce
- ⅓ cup pepperoni
- 2 cups shredded Mozzarella cheese

Instructions:
a) A 12-inch cast-iron pan should be greased.
b) Into the pan, press the gluten-free dough.
c) 3. Add shredded Mozzarella cheese and pepperoni as desired.
d) Bake the pizza at 425°F for 20 to 25 minutes.
e) Cut and present.

115) *Gluten-free Cauliflower crust Pizza*

Indulge in the deliciousness of pizza without the guilt with our Cauliflower Crust Pizza. Perfect for those who prefer gluten-free or low-carb options, this nutritious alternative is a popular choice. Indulge in a guilt-free pizza experience with our innovative recipe that boasts a crust crafted from finely grated cauliflower. Combined with eggs and cheese, this unique dough is sure to tantalize your taste buds and leave you craving for more. Experience the perfect crust - baked to a firm, golden perfection. Indulge in a mouth-watering pizza experience with our freshly baked crust, generously topped with a savory tomato sauce, gooey cheese, and a delectable selection of toppings ranging from crisp vegetables to succulent meats and fragrant herbs. Indulge in a pizza that boasts a delightful lightness, bursting with flavor and offering a gratifying crunch. Indulge in the delectable experience of pizza while incorporating more veggies into your diet with our Cauliflower Crust Pizza. It's the perfect choice for health-conscious foodies who refuse to compromise on taste.

Makes: 1 pizza
Baking Time: 5 minutes

Ingredients:
FOR THE CRUST
- 1 cauliflower head, sliced, cooked, and grated
- 1 teaspoon salt
- 1 teaspoon mixed herbs
- ½ cup Mozzarella cheese
- 1 egg

PIZZA TOPPINGS
- 1 green bell pepper
- ½ cup Mozzarella cheese
- ½ cup cooked mushrooms
- 1 onion
- 2 tablespoons pizza sauce

Instructions
a) Combine the grated cauliflower, egg, mozzarella cheese, salt, and mixed herbs in a bowl.
b) Spread the cauliflower mixture into a perfect circle on a sheet pan that has been lined.
c) Place the crust in a 250°C preheated oven and bake for 15 minutes.
d) After taking the crust out of the oven, spread the pizza sauce over it evenly.
e) Add the toppings of your choice, including sliced green bell pepper, sautéed mushrooms, and sliced onion.
f) Add another minute to the pizza's baking time.
g) Cut and plate.

116) *Gluten-Free BBQ Chicken Pizza*

Indulge in the delicious and fulfilling Gluten-Free BBQ Chicken Pizza, perfect for those who opt for a gluten-free lifestyle. Indulge in a mouth-watering gluten-free pizza crust, generously topped with succulent grilled or roasted chicken, zesty barbecue sauce, and a medley of melted cheeses. Elevate your toppings game with the addition of vibrant red onions, crisp bell peppers, and fragrant fresh cilantro. These ingredients will infuse your dish with an extra burst of flavor and a refreshing touch. Indulge in a mouthwatering pizza that boasts a perfect balance of savory and sweet notes, complemented by the irresistible smokiness of barbecue chicken. Indulge in the mouth-watering flavors of BBQ chicken on a gluten-free pizza crust. Our Gluten-Free BBQ Chicken Pizza is the perfect choice for those seeking a delectable and fulfilling pizza experience without the gluten.

Makes: 8 slices
Baking Time: 20-25 minutes

Ingredients
- 1 recipe gluten-free dough
- ¼ cup grated sharp cheddar cheese
- ¼ cup sliced red onion
- ¼ cup + 2 tablespoons BBQ sauce
- ½ cup shredded Mozzarella cheese
- ¼ cup shredded Monterey Jack cheese
- 2 slices cooked bacon, crumbled
- ½ cup cooked and shredded chicken
- Chopped cilantro

Instructions
a) Prepare the gluten-free dough as directed in the recipe, then bake it for a little period of time.
b) Combine the shredded chicken and two tablespoons of BBQ sauce in a bowl.
c) Evenly spread ¼ cup of BBQ sauce over the half baked crust.
d) Disperse the chicken that has been coated with sauce.
e) Top with grated cheddar cheese, Monterey Jack cheese, and mozzarella cheese.
f) Scatter red onion slices and crumbled bacon over the cheeses.
g) Add another 10 to 15 minutes to the pizza's baking time.
h) Add chopped cilantro as a garnish.
i) Cut and plate

CHAPTER 9: GRILLED PIZZA

117) *Grilled Chicken barbecue pizza*

Indulge in the irresistible blend of smoky grilled flavors and tangy barbecue sauce with our Grilled Chicken Barbecue Pizza. Indulge in the ultimate grilled pizza experience with this mouth-watering recipe. Savory grilled chicken, melted cheese, and a tangy barbecue sauce come together on a perfectly crispy crust to create a flavor explosion that will leave your taste buds begging for more. Enhance your pizza experience with a burst of color and freshness by adding complementary ingredients like red onions, bell peppers, and cilantro to your toppings. Indulge in the perfect balance of savory and sweet with our mouth-watering pizza. Our expertly charred crust and succulent chicken combine to create a delectable contrast of textures that will leave your taste buds begging for more. Elevate your outdoor gatherings and barbecue parties with the mouthwatering Grilled Chicken Barbecue Pizza. This delectable twist on traditional pizza boasts a subtle smoky flavor that will tantalize your taste buds.

Makes: 6 portions
Grilling Time: 3-4 minutes

Ingredients:
- Two 10-inch Quick and Easy Pizza Crusts
- 1 cup grilled, boneless, skinless chicken
- ¼ cup segmented green onion
- ½ cup shredded Smoked Gouda cheese
- ¼ cup diced fresh cilantro
- ⅔ cup barbecue sauce, divided
- ½ cup shredded Mozzarella cheese

Instructions:
a) Add ¼ cup of barbecue sauce to the chicken.
b) Place one crust on a grill rack that has been greased, then cook for 3 minutes.
c) Turn the crust over and cover it with three tablespoons of barbecue sauce.
d) Top with the chicken mixture, mozzarella cheese, green onions, and smoked gouda cheese.
e) Cook the food for 3–4 minutes. Add chopped cilantro on the top.
f) Cut and present.

118) *Grilled ham-and-potato pizzas*

Indulge in the mouth-watering goodness of Grilled Ham-and-Potato Pizzas, where the delectable blend of savory ham, creamy potatoes, and smoky grilled flavors come together in perfect harmony. Indulge in a mouth-watering grilled pizza crust, generously topped with savory thinly sliced ham, tender potato slices, and a layer of ooey-gooey melted cheese. Experience a burst of flavor with our delicious pizza toppings, perfectly complemented by caramelized onions, garlic, and fresh herbs like rosemary or thyme. Indulge in a pizza that is not only filling but also deeply satisfying. The smoky and charred crust sets the stage for a delectable blend of ham and potatoes that will warm your soul. Indulge in the delectable Grilled Ham-and-Potato Pizzas, a perfect choice for those seeking a distinctive and mouth-watering pizza experience that accentuates the classic flavors of a ham and potato dish.

Makes: 1 portion
Grilling Time: 3 minutes

Ingredients:
- 1 recipe for whole-wheat pizza dough
- 1 pound of boiling new potatoes
- 2 cups of shredded Gruyere cheese
- 1 jar of divided pesto sauce
- ¼ cup of diced green onions
- 8 ounces of sliced ham
- ½ tea spoon pepper
- 1 tea spoon salt

Instructions:
a) Roll out the dough to a thickness of ¼ inch on a surface that has been lightly floured, and then cut it into 4 rounds.
b) Grill each round for two to three minutes after brushing it with olive oil on one side.
c) Apply extra olive oil to the tops' greased side.
d) Cut the potatoes into very thin slices and mix them with ¼ cup of pesto.
e) Smear each pizza crust with 1 tablespoon of the potato-pesto mixture.
f) Evenly sprinkling shredded Gruyere cheese, sliced green onions, segmented ham, salt, and pepper over each pizza crust.
g) Grill for 3 minutes at 400°F while it is covered.
h) Cut and present.

119) _Grilled pizza and sausage and salsa_

Experience a fiery and lively take on classic pizza with our Grilled Pizza featuring savory sausage and tangy salsa. The perfect combination of smoky and zesty flavors, this pizza is sure to tantalize your taste buds. Indulge in a mouthwatering grilled pizza crust, adorned with savory slices of grilled sausage, a luscious layer of melted cheese, and a generous serving of fresh, zesty salsa. Experience a burst of freshness and acidity with our salsa, crafted with only the finest ingredients including diced tomatoes, onions, jalapeños, cilantro, and lime juice. Elevate your taste buds with a tantalizing finish of chili flakes or hot sauce to add an extra kick of heat to your toppings. Indulge in a pizza that boasts bold flavors and a smoky, charred crust that sets the perfect foundation for the zesty salsa and spicy sausage toppings. Indulge in the fiery flavors of Grilled Pizza with Sausage and Salsa! Perfect for those who crave a little spice and love to explore the exciting world of grilled pizza.

Makes: 1 serving
Grilling Time: 5 minutes

Ingredients:
- 1 prepared pizza dough
- 1 tablespoon cornmeal
- 1 dish of tomato salsa
- ¾ pound of casing-free chorizo
- Olive oil
- 1 tablespoon seeded and chopped jalapeño chilli
- ¾ cup sliced fresh cilantro
- 1 cup shredded Monterey Jack cheese
- Sour cream with guacamole

Instructions:
a) Cook the pizza crust for 3 minutes on an oiled grill.
b) Flip the crust over and sprinkle cornmeal over the cooked side.
c) Add diced cilantro, diced jalapenos, crumbled chorizo, grated Monterey Jack cheese, and tomato salsa over top.
d) Grill with a cover for about five minutes.
e) Top with sour cream and guacamole.

120) *Grilled sausage- spinach pizzas*

Indulge in the mouth-watering blend of savory sausage and vibrant spinach with our Grilled Sausage and Spinach Pizzas. The smoky flavors of the grill add an extra layer of deliciousness to this already irresistible dish. Indulge in the savory flavors of our grilled pizza crust, adorned with crumbled cooked sausage, a layer of melted cheese, and a generous portion of fresh spinach. Satisfy your cravings with this delectable recipe. Experience the perfect balance of flavors and textures with our grilled pizza topped with fresh spinach. As it cooks, the spinach gently wilts, imparting a subtle earthy flavor and vibrant green hue to every slice. Elevate your taste buds with our delectable selection of toppings, including savory caramelized onions, aromatic garlic, and earthy mushrooms, all designed to add an extra layer of flavor and texture to your dish. Indulge in a pizza that is not only filling but also packed with nutrients. The smoky crust perfectly complements the savory sausage and lively spinach, resulting in a truly delightful experience. Indulge in the delectable Grilled Sausage and Spinach Pizzas - a perfect choice for those seeking a scrumptious and fulfilling grilled pizza that boasts of nutritious ingredients.

Makes: 1 portion
Grilling Time: 2-3 minutes

Ingredients:
- A 32-ounce bag of frozen bread dough;
- A half-pound of hot sausage;
- 2 cups of shredded Monterey Jack cheese
- 1 package of diced spinach
- ½ tea spoon of pepper
- 1 tea spoon of salt

Instructions:
a) After cutting the dough into four circles, roll it out.
b) Place the rounds on a grill that has been oiled and cook for 2 to 3 minutes.
c) Apply 1½ tea spoons of olive oil to the dough rounds' tops.
d) Combine the browned sausage, chopped spinach, pepper, salt, and Monterey Jack cheese in another bowl.
e) Cover the pizza crusts with an even layer of the sausage and spinach mixture.
f) Grill for about 2 minutes at 400°F.
g) Cut and plate.

CHAPTER 10: DEEP-DISH AND PAN PIZZA

121) *Broccoli & Mushroom Dish Pizza*

Indulge in a delectable and wholesome variation of the classic pizza with our Broccoli & Mushroom Dish Pizza. Savor the rich and earthy tones of broccoli and mushrooms that will tantalize your taste buds. Indulge in the ultimate pizza experience with our classic crust recipe, topped with a mouthwatering combination of sautéed broccoli florets, sliced mushrooms, and a delectable blend of melted cheeses. Enhance your pizza experience with a perfect combination of toppings, accompanied by a tantalizing drizzle of olive oil, a delicate sprinkle of garlic, and a touch of red pepper flakes to add a subtle kick of heat. Indulge in a pizza that not only satiates your cravings but also brims with nourishing components. Indulge in the delectable Broccoli & Mushroom Dish Pizza, the perfect pick for those who crave a veggie-packed pizza that doesn't compromise on taste.

Makes: 1 pizza
Baking Time: 30-40 minutes

Ingredients:
- 1 table spoon shortening
- ¼ cup of + 2 table spoons Olive oil
- 1 traditional Italian basic dough
- 1 pound of Italian sausage,
- 12 ounces of canned tomato paste,
- 2 able spoons butter
- 2 tea spoons Oregano
- 2 tea spoons Basil
- 3½ cups of grated mozzarella cheese –
- ½ cup of grated parmesan cheese
- 2 cups of chopped mushrooms
- Crushed teaspoons, three Garlic
- 15 ounces of tomato sauce in a can
- Pepper and salt
- 1 tea spoon finely minced fennel seeds
- 8 cups blanched broccoli

Instructions:
a) Heat ¼ cup of oil in a pan. Cook the garlic for 30 seconds after adding it.
b) Add the basil, oregano, tomato sauce, and tomato paste. Place aside.
c) In a skillet with hot oil, sauté the mushrooms until they are browned and the liquid has cooked off. Place aside.
d) Crumble the Italian sausage, remove the casings, and sauté it with fennel that has been crushed. Place aside.
e) Warm up 1 tea spoon of garlic in 2 table spoons of oil.
f) Stir well after adding the broccoli. Place aside.
g) Spread the dough in a deep dish that has been buttered, letting part of it hang over the sides.
h) To make a raised rim, fold and crimp the pan's edge inward.
i) Top the dough with a tablespoon of oil and a sprinkle of salt.
j) Cover the dough with 1 cup of mozzarella cheese.
k) Arrange the mushrooms and tomatoes on top.
l) Arrange the broccoli on top of the cooked sausage-topped dough.
m) Add the remaining cheeses on top and then drizzle 1/4 cup of oil over them.
n) Bake at 425°F for approximately 35 minutes.

122) _Deep-Dish Pizza_

Indulge in the timeless delight of Deep-Dish Pizza, a beloved classic hailing from the Windy City. Savor the deep, thick, and buttery crust that has made this dish a fan favorite for generations. Indulge in a mouthwatering deep-dish pizza crust that's packed with a hearty blend of ingredients. Indulge in a mouthwatering pizza experience with our signature crust, generously layered with premium mozzarella cheese, and topped with savory Italian sausage, crisp bell peppers, flavorful onions, and a rich tomato sauce. Experience the perfect pizza with a crispy yet soft crust and a deliciously gooey and flavorful interior, baked to perfection. Indulge in the ultimate satisfaction of Deep-Dish Pizza, featuring the unique style and flavors that make Chicago-style pizza a true standout.

Makes: 1 pizza
Baking Time: 1 hour

Ingredients:
- 6 chiffonade cut fresh basil leaves
- ½ cup of pizza sauce
- 1 small conventional pizza dough
- 8 ounces of sliced Pepperoni
- 1 tablespoon of grated Parmesan
- 1 pinch of crushed red pepper
- 8 ounces of sliced mozzarella cheese

Instructions:
a)   Set the slow cooker to high for 20 minutes to pre-heat it.
b)   Cut the dough into a shape like the slow cooker insert by rolling it out.
c)   Insert the dough into the cooker, if required smoothing it out.
d)   On high, cook uncovered for one hour.
e)   Arrange mozzarella slices on top of the crust.
f)   Add pepperoni on top.
g)   Drizzle pizza sauce over the top.
h)   Top with freshly grated Parmesan.
i)   Cook for an additional hour on high.
j)   Using a spatula, carefully remove the pizza from the slow cooker.
k)   Add basil and red pepper flakes as garnish.

123) *Pan Pizza*

Indulge in the mouth-watering and versatile Pan Pizza, renowned for its thick and fluffy crust that boasts a crispy exterior and a tender interior. Experience the perfect pizza with a golden and crispy crust by using a deep pan or skillet with this recipe. Indulge in our signature pizza that boasts a perfectly pressed dough, generously topped with a savory tomato sauce, gooey cheese, and an array of toppings to choose from. Experience the ultimate pizza indulgence with our perfectly baked pizza. Our thick and doughy base is crafted to perfection, while the combination of flavors will tantalize your taste buds. Indulge in the ultimate pizza experience with Pan Pizza! Our delicious pies are guaranteed to satisfy your cravings and provide a comforting meal that both kids and adults will love.

Makes: 1 pizza
Baking Time: 20-25 minutes

Ingredients:
- 1 clove garlic, peeled and chopped
- 1 traditional Italian basic Dough
- 2 tablespoons Tomato paste
- 1 teaspoon Salt
- Pinch of chili flakes
- 128 ounces Canned Crushed tomatoes
- 2 tablespoons Honey
- 2 tablespoons Olive oil

Instructions:
a) Warm up the olive oil in a pan and cook garlic in the pan for two to three minutes.
b) Include a splash of tomato paste and red pepper flakes.
c) Add the tomato paste, then boil for 30 minutes.
d) Use an immersion blender to puree the sauce, then add salt and honey.
e) Use olive oil to coat three baking pans with high sides.
f) Separate the dough into three equal halves.
g) Use your fingers to gently stretch and make dimples in the dough to cover the pans.
h) Spoon four to five table spoons of sauce onto each piece of dough.
i) Add mozzarella and pepperoni on top.
j) Add oregano and sprinkle with extra virgin olive oil.
k) Place the pizzas in a single layer on a baking sheet and bake for 15 to 25 minutes.
l) To inspect the bottoms, lift the pizza with an offset spatula.

124) *Breakfast Skillet Pizza*

Indulge in the mouthwatering Breakfast Skillet Pizza, a savory and delectable take on the classic pizza that is sure to kickstart your day on a high note. Indulge in a breakfast-inspired pizza like no other! Our mouth-watering recipe boasts a crispy crust, generously topped with savory bacon, fluffy scrambled eggs, gooey cheese, and a colorful blend of bell peppers and onions. Elevate your pizza toppings with a final touch of fragrant herbs like chives or parsley, and a tantalizing drizzle of hot sauce or maple syrup for an extra burst of flavor. Experience the perfect fusion of a traditional breakfast and a delicious pizza, all in one easy-to-eat package. Indulge in the Breakfast Skillet Pizza, a delectable choice for pizza enthusiasts craving a morning or mid-morning treat. This savory dish packs a punch, providing a filling and gratifying experience that will energize you for the day ahead.

Makes: 1 pizza
Baking Time: 15-25 minutes

Ingredients:
- 1 chilled crescent roll
- 8 ounces of dough
- 6 eggs
- 1 lb. of ground pork sausage
- ½tea spoon salt
- ½ cup of milk
- 1 tea spoon of freshly cracked black pepper
- 8 ounces of shredded Cheddar cheese

Instructions:
a) Onto an oiled pan, press the crescent roll dough.
b) In a heated skillet, cook the ground pork sausage.
c) Sprinkle sausage and cheddar cheese on top of the crescent roll.
d) Combine the milk, eggs, salt, and pepper in a bowl, then pour the mixture into the baking dish.
e) Bake for about 20 minutes while covered with foil.
f) Bake for a further 15 to 25 minutes after removing the lid.

125) *Chicago Style Pizza*

Experience the legendary and iconic taste of Chicago-Style Pizza, a pizza style that has gained worldwide recognition. Indulge in a mouth-watering deep-dish pizza that's brimming with a medley of toppings. Our signature crust is generously layered with creamy mozzarella cheese, and then piled high with savory Italian sausage, zesty onions, crisp green peppers, and a robust tomato sauce that's sure to tantalize your taste buds. Experience a unique and delicious flavor profile with our expertly crafted pizza, assembled in reverse order with the cheese on the bottom and the sauce on top. Indulge in the irresistible deep-dish crust that boasts a buttery and flaky texture, perfectly crafted to hold the hearty toppings in place. Experience the bold flavors and iconic style of the Windy City with Chicago-Style Pizza - a true indulgence that pizza enthusiasts simply must try.

Makes: 1 pizza
Baking Time: 25 minutes

Ingredients:
- 1 Chicago-style pizza dough
- 1 Green bell pepper, seeded and sliced
- ½ cup diced Canadian bacon
- ½ cup diced Ham
- 2 ounces grated Parmesan cheese
- 1 Onion, sliced
- ¼ pound crumbled and cooked Pork Sausage
- ½ pound crumbled and cooked Ground beef
- ¼ pound crumbled and cooked Italian Sausage
- 12 ounces shredded Mozzarella cheese
- 1 cup Pizza sauce
- ½ cup diced Pepperoni
- ¼ pound sliced Mushrooms

Instructions:
a) Set the oven for pizza at 475°F.
b) Create a 13-inch round out of the dough.
c) Fold the extra dough to form a rim and layer the dough on a pizza pan that has been greased.
d) After applying the pizza sauce, completely cover the top with mozzarella cheese.
e) Place the vegetables and meats on top.
f) The pizza should bake for around 25 minutes.

126) *Deep Dish Porchetta Pizza*

Indulge in the ultimate culinary fusion with our Deep Dish Porchetta Pizza. Savor the delectable combination of two beloved traditions - the rich flavors of deep-dish pizza and the succulent taste of Italian-style roasted pork, also known as porchetta. Get ready to tantalize your taste buds with every bite. Indulge in a mouthwatering deep-dish pizza crust that is generously topped with slices of succulent and savory porchetta, smothered in a layer of melted cheese, and finished off with a tangy tomato sauce. Experience the ultimate pizza indulgence with our expertly crafted pies. Our pizzas are baked to perfection, ensuring a delectable blend of textures and flavors that will tantalize your taste buds. The crust is expertly crafted to achieve a golden, crispy finish that will leave you craving for more. Indulge in the perfect pairing of rich and savory porchetta with cheesy and saucy components, resulting in a truly satisfying pizza experience. Indulge in the savory and mouth-watering Deep Dish Porchetta Pizza, perfect for those seeking to add a touch of Italian sophistication to their pizza palate. Savor the succulent pork goodness that will leave your taste buds craving for more.

Makes: 4 servings
Baking Time: 20-25 minutes

Ingredients:
DEEP DISH DOUGH
- 3½ cups Flour
- 1 pinch Salt
- 1 cup slightly boiled Water
- ¾ ounces Brewer's yeast
- ¾ ounce Lard

TOPPINGS
- ¾ cup peeled and chopped Tomatoes
- ¾ cup sliced Potato
- ¼ pound thinly sliced Porchetta
- Onion
- Sliced Raspadura cheese
- Extra virgin olive oil
- Oregano

Instructions:
a) Combine the dough's components.
b) Place the dough in a round, oiled pan with a rim and give it a good kneading.
c) Top the dough with salt, oregano, and tomatoes. Let it ascend.
d) In a pan with two table spoons of oil, cook the potatoes for 6 minutes.
e) Continue cooking for a further 2 minutes after adding salt and half of an onion.
f) Place the potatoes and onions on top of the dough when it has risen.
g) Bake at 350 degrees Fahrenheit for 20 to 25 minutes.
h) Plate with sliced porchetta and raspadura cheese.

CHAPTER 11: PITA PIZZA

127) *Pita pizza with green olives*

Indulge in a mouth-watering pizza experience with our Pita Pizza topped with savory Green Olives. Savor the deliciousness of this quick and easy meal option that's bursting with flavor. Discover the ultimate pizza hack with our recipe that utilizes pita bread as the perfect crust. Enjoy the convenience of a ready-made base that's both delicious and easy to work with. Indulge in our mouth-watering pita bread, generously topped with zesty tomato sauce, a rich layer of mozzarella cheese, and a vibrant combination of green olives. Experience a burst of flavor with our delicious pizza topped with briny and tangy olives that add the perfect amount of saltiness to every bite. Experience the perfect balance of flavors with our expertly crafted toppings, finished with a sprinkle of fragrant herbs like oregano or basil. Indulge in the ultimate customizable treat with our Pita Pizza featuring delicious green olives. Perfect for a quick lunch or a satisfying snack, this versatile option can be tailored to your unique taste buds.

Makes: 4 pizzas
Baking Time: 10 minutes

Ingredients:
- Flakes of red pepper (if desired)
- Four 7-inch pita flatbread without pockets
- One cup of salad, chopped
- grated Monterey Jack cheese, 8 ounces
- pitted and chopped green olives in a half-cup
- black pepper freshly cracked
- 2 chopped jalapeo peppers
- Parmesan cheese shaved as a garnish

Instructions:
a) To 450°F, preheat the pizza oven.
b) Bake the pita bread for three minutes on a heated pizza stone or griddle.
c) Combine the grated cheese, chopped jalapenos, and green olives in a bowl.
d) Spread the cheese and olive mixture evenly across the four pitas.
e) Until the cheese is melted and bubbling, bake for 5 minutes.
f) Pizzas should be topped with chopped salad and shaved Parmesan cheese.
g) In a 400 degree oven, bake or grill the pizzas for an additional 10 minutes.

128) *Lunchbox Pita Pizza*

Introducing the Lunchbox Pita Pizza - the ultimate solution for busy parents and their little ones! This delicious and easy-to-eat option is perfect for packing in lunchboxes or enjoying as a quick meal on-the-go. Experience the ultimate convenience with our pizza recipe that features pita bread as the crust. Its compact and portable base makes it the perfect on-the-go meal. Indulge in our mouth-watering pita bread, generously topped with a savory tomato sauce, a luscious layer of mozzarella cheese, and an array of your favorite toppings to satisfy your cravings. Indulge in a delicious lunchtime treat with our mouth-watering pita pizza options. Choose from classic pepperoni, fresh diced bell peppers, juicy sliced cherry tomatoes, or savory mushrooms to create the perfect lunchbox meal. Our toppings are carefully selected to cater to the young ones' palates, keeping them simple yet irresistible. Introducing our mini pizza - the ultimate solution for your busy school days or picnics. With its mouth-watering flavor and easy-to-eat size, you'll never have to compromise on taste or convenience again. Introducing the Lunchbox Pita Pizza - a delicious and hassle-free meal that's sure to win over both young and old taste buds.

Makes: 1 pizza
Baking Time: 5 minutes

Ingredients:

- Salt with garlic, 1/8 tea spoon
- Sliced Crimini mushrooms, 1 cup
- Pizza sauce, 3 tablespoons
- Shredded mozzarella cheese in 12 cups
- One circular pita bread
- Olive oil, 1 teaspoon

Instructions:

a) A grill should be preheated and lightly greased.
b) On one half of the pita, spread pizza sauce and olive oil.
c) On top, arrange the garlic salt, sliced mushrooms, and shredded mozzarella cheese.
d) Pizza made with pitas should be placed on the grill and covered.
e) Grill the cheese until it is melted and bubbling for about five minutes.

129) *Greek Style Pita Pizza*

Indulge in the rich and vibrant flavors of Greek cuisine with our Greek-Style Pita Pizza. This Mediterranean twist on traditional pizza is sure to tantalize your taste buds and leave you craving for more. Indulge in a delectable pizza experience with our recipe that boasts a unique twist - pita bread as the crust. The result? A light and crispy base that will tantalize your taste buds. Indulge in the savory flavors of our pita bread, smothered in a zesty tomato sauce and generously sprinkled with crumbled feta cheese. Our Greek-inspired toppings add the perfect finishing touch to this mouthwatering dish. Indulge in the deliciousness of Greek-style pita pizza with classic toppings like kalamata olives, red onions, diced tomatoes, and a dash of dried oregano. Experience the taste of the Mediterranean with our delicious blend of salty feta cheese, tangy tomatoes, and savory olives. This delightful combination of flavors will transport you to the sun-soaked Greek islands with every bite. Indulge in the refreshing and flavorful Greek-Style Pita Pizza, a perfect option that brings the taste of the Mediterranean straight to your plate.

Makes: 4 pita pizzas
Baking Time: 10 minutes

Ingredients
- ½ onion, sliced
- Pizza sauce, One cup
- 10 Kalamata olives, pitted and sliced
- Mozzarella, 7 ounces
- Four pita bread
- Feta cheese, crumbled, 7 ounces
- 1 tomato, diced
- 1 green bell pepper, and sliced

Instructions
a) Set the oven's temperature to 375 degrees Fahrenheit.
b) On a baking sheet, arrange the pita bread.
c) Each pita should be spread with pizza sauce and topped with mozzarella cheese.
d) On top, strew the chopped onions, sliced tomatoes, and crumbled feta cheese.
e) Green bell peppers and Kalamata olives should be added.
f) Until the cheese is melted and bubbling, bake for 10 minutes.

130) *Artichoke & Prosciutto Pita Pizza*

Indulge in a gourmet-inspired dish with our Pita Pizza featuring the rich and savory flavors of artichokes and prosciutto. Discover the ultimate pizza hack with our recipe that uses pita bread as the crust. This convenient and versatile base will elevate your pizza game to the next level. Indulge in our mouth-watering pita bread, generously topped with a luscious garlic sauce, melted mozzarella cheese, and a delectable mix of marinated artichoke hearts and thinly sliced prosciutto. Experience the earthy flavor of artichokes and the rich, salty taste of prosciutto on our delicious pizza. Elevate your pizza experience with a final touch of freshly sprinkled basil or arugula, imparting a burst of vibrant and herbaceous flavor to your taste buds. Indulge in the exquisite taste of Pita Pizza with Artichokes and Prosciutto - a sophisticated and flavorful option that is guaranteed to impress your guests or elevate your weeknight dinner.

Makes: 4 pizzas
Baking Time: 5 minutes

Ingredients
- Chopped artichoke hearts
- Red onion, sliced
- Shredded mozzarella cheese, One cup
- Fresh basil, for garnish

- Prosciutto
- Roasted Red Pepper Sauce, One cup
- Parmesan cheese, Half a cup, Grated
- Roasted red peppers

Instructions
a) Set the oven's temperature to 450 degrees Fahrenheit.
b) Apply a thin layer of olive oil to the pita bread's both surfaces.
c) Each pita should be covered with roasted red pepper sauce and shredded mozzarella cheese.
d) Add sliced red onion, chopped artichoke hearts, and prosciutto on top.
e) On top, grate some Parmesan cheese and scatter some roasted red peppers.
f) Until the cheese is melted and bubbling, bake for 5 minutes.
g) Pizzas should be served with fresh basil on top.

CONCLUSION

Pizza has been a significant part of Italian heritage and culture since the sixteenth century. It has spread worldwide and has been embraced, adapted, and enjoyed by people from different backgrounds.

When it comes to making pizza, having experience is important, but equally important is selecting the right ingredients and quantities. If you're a pizza enthusiast, you can recreate these amazing recipes at home and savor the authentic flavors. By following tradition carefully, you'll be able to enjoy any type of pizza you desire, ensuring the best possible outcome.

ALPHABETICAL INDEX

Made in United States
Troutdale, OR
10/10/2023

13580576R00075